Curves to the Apple

THE REPRODUCTION OF PROFILES

LAWN OF EXCLUDED MIDDLE

RELUCTANT GRAVITIES

Also by Rosmarie Waldrop

POETRY

The Aggressive Ways of the Casual Stranger (Random House)

The Road Is Everywhere or Stop This Body (Open Places)

When They Have Senses (Burning Deck)

Nothing Has Changed (Awede)

Streets Enough to Welcome Snow (Station Hill)

The Reproduction of Profiles (New Directions)

Shorter American Memory (Paradigm Press)

Peculiar Motions (Kelsey St. Press)

Lawn of Excluded Middle (Tender Buttons)

A Key Into the Language of America (New Directions)

Another Language: Selected Poems (Talisman House)

Differences for Four Hands (Singing Horse Press /
2nd ed. Paradigm Press)

Split Infinites (Singing Horse Press)

Blindsight (New Directions)

Love, like Pronouns (Omnidawn)

Splitting Image (Zasterle)

WITH KEITH WALDROP

Well Well Reality (Post-Apollo Press)

FICTION

The Hanky of Pippin's Daughter (Station Hill)

A Form/ of Taking/ It All (Station Hill)

TRANSLATIONS

The Book of Questions by Edmond Jabès
(Wesleyan University Press)

The Book of Resemblances by Edmond Jabès
(Wesleyan University Press)

The Book of Dialogue by Edmond Jabès
(Wesleyan University Press)

From the Book to the Book: an Edmond Jabès Reader
(Wesleyan University Press)

Curves to the Apple

THE REPRODUCTION OF PROFILES

LAWN OF EXCLUDED MIDDLE

RELUCTANT GRAVITIES

BY **ROSMARIE WALDROP**

A New Directions Book

Acknowledgments for individual volumes appear on page 196.

Manufactured in the United Sates of America
First published as New Directions Paperbook 1046 in 2006
Book design by Sylvia Frezzolini Severance, Westerly, Rhode Island

Library of Congress Cataloging-in-Publication Data

Waldrop, Rosmarie.
  Curves to the apple / by Rosmarie Waldrop.
    p. cm.
  ISBN-13: 978-0-8112-1673-9 (pbk. : acid-free paper)
  ISBN-10: 0-8112-1673-X (pbk. : acid-free paper)
  I. Title.
  PS3573.A4234C87 2006
  811'.54—dc22

                              2006019328

10 9 8

New Directions Books are published for James Laughlin
by New Directions Publishing Corporation
80 Eighth Avenue, New York, NY 10011

for Keith Waldrop

CONTENTS

INTRODUCTION

Just as the title, *Curves to the Apple*, evokes both the organic and the geometric (not to mention myth and the history of science) the poems of this trilogy try to navigate conflicting, but inextricable, claims of body and mind, feeling and logic.

Usually, when I finish a sequence of poems, it is the end of a world. I enter what Edmond Jabès called "The Book of Torment," the space between projects where it seems uncertain that one will ever write again. But after finishing *The Reproduction of Profiles* I kept being haunted by some of its phrases, like "all resonance grows from consent to emptiness." The fact that the "empty" space inside a flute or violin is where the sound happens, and that the uterus, a likewise "empty" organ, is a locus of fertility wanted to be thought about.

No doubt I was attuned to this idea of an empty center because I had been translating the seven volumes of Edmond Jabès's *Book of Questions*, a work that keeps turning around an empty transcendence, a non-existent God.

This was not a direction I could go. For me, the theme connected rather with the law of excluded middle. I had used — and misused — Wittgenstein phrases all through *The Reproduction of Profiles*. I could now happily continue trying to subvert the authority, the closure, of logical propositions and explore the fertile "lawn" between true and false, black and white.

My playing field was widened when I read A. S. Eddington's *The Nature of the Physical World*. The picture of the world drawn by classical physics conflicts with the picture drawn by quantum theory. As Eddington says, we use classical physics on Monday, Wednesday, Friday, and quantum theory on Tuesday, Thursday, Saturday.

I continued in the form of the prose poem which for me has come to fit Pound's postulate of "a center around which, not a box within which." I also continued with the dialogue between an "I" and a "you." These tend to be taken as the voices of a man and a woman because gender stereotypes are played with in the poems. They can also be the two voices in everybody's inner dialogue. For me, they are grammatical, as is the lyrical "I." This "I" has lately been confused with the expression of unquestioned subjectivity and identity. But it simply indicates that language is taking place.

However, the rhetorical "you" had hardly a chance against the dominant "I" in these two books. For the third volume, *Reluctant Gravities*, I decided that the two voices should be given equal space. Again, the two voices do not so much represent characters as frame the synaptic space between them. So the trajectory of the three volumes of the trilogy might be from "the empty space I place in the center of each poem to allow penetration" to the "ultimate gap, as between two people, that not even a penis can bridge."

—Rosmarie Waldrop
May, 2006

Curves to the Apple

THE REPRODUCTION
OF PROFILES

■ ■ ■ ■ ■ ■

PART ONE

THE REPRODUCTION OF PROFILES

I had inferred from pictures that the world was real and therefore paused, for who knows what will happen if we talk truth while climbing the stairs. In fact, I was afraid of following the picture to where it reaches right out into reality, laid against it like a ruler. I thought I would die if my name didn't touch me, or only with its very end, leaving the inside open to so many feelers like chance rain pouring down from the clouds. You laughed and told everybody that I had mistaken the Tower of Babel for Noah in his Drunkenness.

I didn't want to take this street which would lead me back home, by my own cold hand, or your advice to find some other man to hold me because studying one headache would not solve the problem of sensation. All this time, I was trying to think, but the river and the bank fused into common darkness, and words took on meanings that made them hard to use in daylight. I believed entropy meant hugging my legs close to my body so that the shadow of the bridge over the Seekonk could be written into the hub of its abandoned swivel.

The proportion of accident in my picture of the world falls with the rain. Sometimes, at night, diluted air. You told me that the poorer houses down by the river still mark the level of the flood, but the world divides into facts like surprised wanderers disheveled by a sudden wind. When you stopped preparing quotes from the ancient misogynists it was clear that you would soon forget my street.

I had already studied mathematics, a mad kind of horizontal reasoning like a landscape that exists entirely on its own, when it is more natural to lie in the grass and make love, glistening, the whole length of the river. Because small, noisy waves, as from strenuous walking, pounded in my ears, I stopped my bleak Saturday, while a great many dry leaves dropped from the sycamore. This possibility must have been in color from the beginning.

Flooding with impulse refracts the body and does not equal. Duck wings opened, jeweled, ablaze in oblique flight. Though a speck in the visual field must have some color, it need not be red. Or beautiful. A mountain throwing its shadow over so much nakedness, or a cloud lighting its edges on the sun, it drowned my breath more deeply, and things lost their simple lines to possibility. Like old idols, you said, which we no longer adore and throw into the current to drift where they still

Only in connection with a body does a shadow make sense. I called mine a dog, the way it ran ahead of me in the dust, breathing rapidly and sticking its small head out in front—though there are intervals where the light stands still, and the air does not resist. Abandoned in my body, the memory of houses at a certain distance, their roofs, and their chimneys for the dark to flow down in arbitrary conventions. This is why you don't like me to get drunk. I fall asleep in the street, without even a shadow to lie on, and crowds gather, afraid of being disappointed.

Was it the jokes you told? Our bodies fitted one another like the links of a chain resplendent with cymbals and xylophones. Because form is the possibility of structure, you hoped there were people watching. My desire was more like a sailor's rolling gait, as if shifting my weight from one side to the other were a matter heavy with consequence. The salt reached saturation. You said wet was wet, without following the river farther than this sentence or looking at negative facts, their non-existent mouths twisted for explanation.

I was not sure I had understood. I was naked enough to disappear in the shop windows. Your weight on me sank through my bones, and I didn't know where I had lost my body—as if it had no vowels, as if the construction were faulty, the mesh too coarse—when you felt a sneeze coming on and fumbled for your handkerchief. I traced the law of sufficient reason down your spine. Your skin was delicate, like a retracted confession.

Everything that can be thought at all, you said, can be thought over. When I asked if you were referring to nuclear arms, genetic engineering, or marriage, you hastily closed the window. I had seen you, in the park, push a banana peel off the sandal of Constance Witherby's statue and recite with large gestures: a poem? a funeral oration? I was not musician enough to read this score, not with the wind blowing your hair against the approach of winter, though if the swallows had stopped circling high in the solid blue, my breath would already have failed me. Sharp smell of the sea, of fish rocking in the surf. And already clouds. You said it might be different if we were able to stand outside logic. I knew by this you meant: barefoot.

For years already, the countryside had been in competition with my thoughts, not like weather moving through the lungs, but pulling. It was beautiful. It wanted to be looked at. And my attention swayed like a poplar in the wind. Nevertheless I had learned to substitute "freedom of the will" for not knowing which future would undress me and pretended to be happy to hold my breath. So I agreed, you said, that there were languages to be admired rather than understood, and that my smiles shot dubious appeals to the passage of time though we knew the river flowed a few yards off whether we tried to cross it or not. The trees rocked gently in the fine mist. Mostly, I had to admit, I live in the subjunctive, unable to find a foothold. If objects were doors, I might be drawn north to forget them.

Waves can be resolved into a statement about unalterable form. It goes without saying they lap at your chin while you are still describing the dangers of dry land, after having loved it so long. The gulls stood still, though the light fell on their strained bodies. They could not be proved within the substance of the world, you said. So different their flight. I was happy to discover cause, the better to ignore effects. The clouds drowned silently in their reflection, pulling water down with them.

We were approaching winter like an object which cannot be put between words. Behavior became simpler since we had dislocated our memories. Still, much was. A little confusion in the propositions will allow for this. Or truth can be so strenuous it makes you lean against the window frame. I thought of breathing deeply to find Venus reflected in the river. Then I would know if standing beside you leaves my lips dry. But I was really dissecting your name by means of definitions which would point the way to the missing copula where I could see the sky. Though the clouds could be uttered in a variety of tones, the stars formed constellations analyzed completely. You cried for the moon, which had started to wane in agreement with constant and variable. What this silver sliver failed to reveal, its expression between my thighs would clarify.

There were obstacles, no doubt about it. Take the huge plain rising against the sky and which we must cross while all we have done in our sleep falls away. Then stipulate singing. If I fail to deposit a coin, everyday language produces the most fundamental confusions, but what pleasure in getting lost if it is unavoidable? Fear, possibly. A vague distance instead of horizon. You were wondering if the same path could be taken by two people. And if any grass had grown on the runway since J. F. Kennedy's take-off.

You told me, if something is not used it is meaningless, and took my temperature which I had thought to save for a more difficult day. In the mirror, every night, the same face, a bit more threadbare, a dress worn too long. The moon was out in the cold, along with the restless, dissatisfied wind that seemed to change the location of the sycamores. I expected reproaches because I had mentioned the word love, but you only accused me of stealing your pencil, and sadness disappeared with sense. You made a ceremony out of holding your head in your hands because, you said, it could not be contained in itself.

If we could just go on walking through these woods and let the pine branches brush our faces, living would still make beads of sweat on your forehead, but you wouldn't have to worry about what you call my exhibitionism. All you liked about trees was the way the light came through the leaves in sheets of precise, parallel rays, like slant rain. This may be an incomplete explanation of our relation, but we've always feared the dark inside the body. You agree there could be no seduction if the structures of propositions did not stand in a physical relation, so that we could get from one to the other. Even so, not every moment of happiness is to hang one's clothes on.

I might have known you wouldn't talk to me. But to claim you just didn't want to disguise your thoughts! We've walked along this road before, I said, though perhaps in heavier coats not designed to reveal the form of the body. Later, the moon came out and threw the shadows of branches across the street where they remained, broken. Feverishly you examined the tacit conventions on which conversation depends. I sighed as one does at night, looking down into the river. I wondered if by throwing myself in I could penetrate to the essence of its character, or should I wait for you to stab me as you had practiced in your dream? You said this question, like most philosophical problems, arose from failing to understand the tale of the two youths, two horses, and two lilies. You could prove to me that the deepest rivers are, in fact, no rivers at all.

From this observation we turned to consider passion. Looking at the glints of light on the water, you tried to make me tell you not to risk the excitement—to recommend cold baths. The lack of certainty, of direction, of duration, was its own argument, unlike going into a bar to get drunk and getting drunk. Your face was alternately hot and cold, as if translating one language into another—gusts from the storm in your heart, the pink ribbon in your pocket. Its actual color turned out to be unimportant, but its presence disclosed something essential about membranes. You said there was still time, you could still break it off, go abroad, make a movie. I said (politely, I thought) this wouldn't help you. You'd have to kill yourself.

Tearing your shirt open, you drew my attention to three dogs in a knot. This served to show how something general can be recorded in unpedigreed notation. I pointed to a bench by a willow, from which we could see the gas tanks across the river, because I thought a bench was a simple possibility: one could sit on it. The black hulks of the tanks began to sharpen in the cold dawn light, though when you leaned against the railing I could smell your hair, which ended in a clean round line on your neck, as was the fashion that year. I had always resented how nimble your neck became whenever you met a woman, regardless of rain falling outside or other calamities. Now, at least, you hunched your shoulders against the shadow of doubt.

This time of day, hesitation can mean tottering on the edge, just before the water breaks into the steep rush and spray of the fall. What could I do but turn with the current and get choked by my inner speed? You tried to breathe against the acceleration, waiting for the air to consent. All the while, we behaved as if this search for a pace were useful, like reaching for a plank or wearing raincoats. I was afraid we would die before we could make a statement, but you said that language presupposed meaning, which would be swallowed by the roar of the waterfall.

Toward morning, walking along the river, you tossed simple objects into the air which was indifferent around us, though it moved off a little, and again as you put your hand back in your pocket to test the degree of hardness. Everything else remained the same. This is why, you said, there was no fiction.

In order to understand the nature of language you began to paint, thinking that the logic of reference would become evident once you could settle the quarrels of point, line, and color. I was distracted from sliding words along the scales of significance by smoke on my margin of breath. I waited for the flame, the passage from eye to world. At dawn, you crawled into bed, exhausted, warning me against drawing inferences across blind canvas. I ventured that a line might represent a tower that would reach the sky, or, on the other hand, rain falling. You replied that the world was already taking up too much space.

Two sailors throwing dice on the quay will not make a monument, but there you sat reading a paper in its shadow. You said once we had a language in which everything was alright, everything would be alright, and your body looked beautiful while a fisherman tied his boat to a post, looping his rope through the metal rings without getting entangled in problems of representation or reflection. Nobody looked at you except for the water which, though it has no shape, is heavy with mirroring that of others. These images, however, are hard to get hold of, sunk as they are at the bottom of the alphabet.

The shifting use of the word "home" corresponds to dim light. A clothesline with pieces of torn underwear, reflected in a puddle. I stood in the yard looking for clues, a cat on the banister, the tick of a clock from years ago. Even as a memory the house was dark. Impossible to distinguish forms on the tip of my tongue. Cold, the closed door, the steps leading up to it. As I was listening at a distance I could only hear the distance. It pulsed in my ears, and the longer I waited the more it. This brings us again, you said, to the vexed question whether desires are internal or more like foreign countries.

At first sight, it did not look like a picture of your body. Any more than the fog rolling in from the sea, covering and uncovering the surface of the river, seemed an extreme. I made excuses for your hesitation because I thought you wanted to contain everything, unimpaired by spelling errors. Then I saw you were trying to lean against the weight of missing words, a wall at the end of the world. But I knew, though it tired me to imagine even a fraction of the distance, that it continued at least as far as one can run from danger, where two women had been washed up on a delay. Neither words nor the rigor of sentences, you said, could stem the steady acceleration of the past.

As the streets were empty in the early morning, I had made the spaces between words broad enough for a smile which could reflect off the enamel tower clock. Being late is one of my essential properties. Unthinkable that I should not possess it, and not even on vacation do I deprive myself of its advantages. Nevertheless I cannot recall a time when I did not try to hide this by changing the shape of my mouth and appearing breathless. The sky was shading from hesitant to harsh, which was not bound to correspond to any one color or tableau vivant. The climate is rainy, no doubt about it, and ready to draw its curtain over my clauses and conjunctions. But what if I had made the spaces too wide to reach the next word and the silence

The Seekonk was losing its shape, flooding, forming a sea of its own by way of experiment. You thought if we stopped making pictures, the word "I" would be terrifying with vagueness, and a massive silence would spread through all the algae and ruined crops. We'd stagnate in puddles, without elegance or variety, before drying into thin sleep. Nothing could drink its fill from our lacking sentences, because if a river has no movement no tales are left dreaming in it. All this time, I tried to describe a blot of ink on white paper by stating for each point on the sheet whether it was black or white.

I had tried to find ways of escaping my daily chores, but then read the river from one bank to the other and took longer. The words must already have sense. They could not acquire it through reflection no matter how strenuous the pigment. Indeed, the light came on inside, to reveal the waters of childhood carrying their junks and packets. If I could only accept similes, you began, but I interrupted with a question about your body of doctrine. That, you said, would take rhythm and logic in afternoon rotation. You preferred to speak of years that pour down like whiskey.

The fog was not dense enough to hide what I didn't want to see, nor did analysis resolve our inner similarities. When you took the knife out of your pocket and stuck it into your upper arm you did not tell me that, if the laws of nature do not explain the world, they still continue its spine. There was no wind, the branches motionless around the bench, a dark scaffolding. A few drops of blood oozed from your wound. I began to suck it, thinking that, because language is part of the human organism, a life could end as an abrupt, violent sentence, or be drawn out with economy into fall and winter, no less complicated than a set of open parentheses from a wrong turn to the shock of under-standing our own desires.

The party began to break up though you were still looking for a point of view by examining thoughts for possible sexual characteristics. People assured one another it had been a nice evasion, when the floor that slanted downward in the mirror was suddenly pulled up to the surface on which you stood, disheveled and exhausted. I understood your desire to communicate, but stepped over it because I was thirsty. I had meant to tell you that it is improper to speak of sex to a person drinking cognac, but not even sober could I have handed you a sequence of missing links.

We can now talk about formal sex in the same sense that we speak of formal concepts, you roared with violent gallantry, but this woman, my God! She was showing us downstairs. At the door, she pressed her body against yours and pressed and pressed until I put a quarter in her hand. Then she covered her mouth as if in fright or in order to protect the wet impact of your lips or, again, to keep a cry from rising into the air on large, trembling wings. I introduce this metaphor in order to get to the source of your confusion between formal sex and sex proper, which has looped the whole of traditional philosophy to the moment, toward the end of day, when the equator embraces the torrid zone.

I could see sleepiness round your skinny limbs, so many dreams cling-
ing to the bone, as I knocked on wood, and the door opened onto the
cold. When snow falls under this category we must advance carefully,
with small steps. But a large moon now lit up the sky which seemed
more navigable for its occasional cloud. Twice I reached out to take
your hand, but as you paid no attention I put mine back in my pocket
until further need. I moved on to saying your name, which shows that
it's easier to label a cold front than to predict the wedding. You said, the
total number of objects was already breathless with growing pains.

You said I should have let her kiss me, too. But now it was too late, my
hand cold as an absence we don't doubt because our understanding so
palpably depends on it. I knew all I could do was go home and smoth-
er my thoughts under my blanket as one does when one sleeps alone.
Then dreams carry the body from the shadow line into a brief splendor,
and China could not be less remote. I thought I would call you a joker
for the hold it would take in your backbone and tease you on. You said,
a dream was a truth like any other, but to outstrip an adversary with tau-
tologies which, as we know, vanish inside themselves, was an extreme
case of provoking phantoms.

Nail clippings have, thanks to Sigmund Freud, become mysterious again, you continued, whereas a proposition flaunts every logical scratch that follows from it. I felt sleepy, no doubt because I have a long past and don't speak foreign languages. The shadows made the ground sink a calculable distance. The dark helps, I said. Open your hands, and there is time in the depth of memory—a mirror with ambition—which assures both interval and continuity by letting slow breathing rise to the surface. Making a smooth stone skim across the water, you replied that the relation of a policeman to a crime about to take place could not be inferred from polluted air. Causality was only one way of losing the world.

You were leaning over the parapet. Night allowed us to see as far back as Roger Williams' landing and the anger which scraped faces off the dead. So much unsolved memory under the bridge. My thoughts began to share the darkness of the river, though we were miles from the nearest reactor. Tips of grass stuck up through the snow. You suddenly smiled into the latency between us and said that her breasts were very white. I felt I ought either to wash this episode out of my centerfold or kiss you for having so little use for me.

Snowflakes floated to the ground with infinite caution, accumulating a silence into which one could not introduce primitive discrepancies. I listened to the muffled thud of our steps and wondered why I could not keep pace with you, even though I clearly saw your feet. You said that "one plus one at midnight equals two" was as nonsensical as a nephrite worn as a charm against kidney stones or a day without birds. A woman opened her window and overlooked the difference between the sexes while you complained that the Milky Way, albeit invisible at the moment, was caused by another long proposition, not unlike amnesia.

It was easier to walk in the snow if I made swimming motions, so I let the moonlight frisk my body which it threatened to reduce to a mere projection. Your body seemed to flicker as you told me how the insides of her thighs lay peacefully in the mirror with no thought for conse-quences. Suppose, I said patiently, kicking at a snowdrift, I am given all the details at once. Then I could construct all possible stories out of them, and that would be the end of it. Annoyed, you bit your native tongue. But I knew well enough that if one leaves things alone they get less clear by themselves.

You were walking ahead, humming Berlioz to keep me from introducing more conditional clauses, from which anything might follow. I predicted your approximate indifference, should I simply take a side street home. Instead, I took a sharp breath and held it, letting the cold melt in my lungs like distance. It brought you skidding toward me on the snow. Winking, you asked: if a heart was infinitely complex, so that its every desire was for infinitely many stiffenings with infinitely many terrors, rather than for risking that a single scream ravage all memory, was such a heart not implausible with ambition and therefore bound to succeed? I said a complete description of the world was given by listing one's fears and then listing one's fulcrums, but you were mocking from the back of a mirror, the silver of multiplication.

Then you came out with how you had jumped her and, trembling with courage, ridden up the hill into the interior, a landscape with something unfinished about it. I was tempted to register doubts as your description progressed, but the wind died down. Cold, at this hour. The moon sank among the clouds as into a lake. A large bird, an owl perhaps, swooped from a tree, and we expected to see it fly up again, its silhouette bulging with prey. Instead, we saw another bird swoop down and, after a while, another. Regardless whether it was several owls or the same, you said, they could be arranged on the road and treated as outlaws of probability. But I hesitated, for fear of not encountering.

It is clear that distance devours the variables and leaves us with all propositions saying the same thing, but with such force that the desire takes us out of body. Tell me that she is beautiful, you demanded, even though you knew that I had always been pleased to lead you astray. A name, I said, cannot go from mouth to mouth, a clear mirror unclouded by breath. Remember that nightingales sing only in the upper pay scales. And we can't logically correlate a fact with a soul, even if fiction sustains the tone of our muscles. Your lips trembled slightly as you said that logic could take care of itself.

■ ■ ■ ■ ■ ■

PART TWO

INSERTING THE MIRROR

1 To explore the nature of rain I opened the door because inside the workings of language clear vision is impossible. You think you see, but are only running your finger through pubic hair. The rain was heavy enough to fall into this narrow street and pull shreds of cloud down with it. I expected the drops to strike my skin like a keyboard. But I only got wet. When there is no resonance, are you more likely to catch a cold? Maybe it was the uniform appearance of the drops which made their application to philosophy so difficult even though the street was full of reflection. In the same way, fainting can, as it approaches, slow the Yankee Doodle to a near loss of pitch. I watched the outline of the tower grow dim until it was only a word in my brain. That language can suggest a body where there is none. Or does a body always contain its own absence? The rain, I thought, ought to protect me against such arid speculations.

2 The body is useful. I can send it on errands while I stay in bed and pull the blue blanket up to my neck. Once I coaxed it to get married. It trembled and cried on the way to the altar, but then gently pushed the groom down to the floor and sat on him while the family crowded closer to get in on the excitement. The black and white flagstones seemed to be rocking, though more slowly than people could see, which made their gestures uncertain. Many of them slipped and lay down. Because they closed their eyes in the hope of opening their bodies I rekindled the attentions of love. High-tension wires very different from propensity and yet again from mirror images. Even if we could not remember the color of heat the dominant fuel would still consume us.

3 Androgynous instinct is one kind of complexity, another is, for example, a group of men crowding into a bar while their umbrellas protect them against the neon light falling. How bent their backs are, I thought. They know it is useless to look up—as if the dusk could balance both a glass and a horizon—or to wonder if the verb "to sleep" is active or passive. When a name has detached itself, its object, ungraspable like everyday life, spills over. A solution not ready to be taken home, splashing heat through our bodies and decimal points.

4 I tried to understand the mystery of names by staring into the mirror and repeating mine over and over. Or the word "me." As if one could come into language as into a room. Lost in the blank, my obsessive detachment spiraled out into the unusable space of infinity, indifferent nakedness. I sat down in it. No balcony for clearer view, but I could focus on the silvered lack of substance or the syllables that correspond to it because all resonance grows from consent to emptiness. But maybe, in my craving for hinges, I confused identity with someone else.

CURVES TO THE APPLE

5 Way down the deserted street, I thought I saw a bus which, with luck, might get me out of this sentence which might go on forever, knotting phrase onto phrase with fire hydrants and parking meters, and still not take me to my language waiting, surely, around some corner. Though I am not certain what to expect. This time it might be Narragansett. Or black. A sidewalk is a narrow location in history, and no bright remarks can hold back the dark. In the same way, when a child throws her ball there is no winning or losing unless she can't remember her name because, although the street lamp has blushed on pink the dark sits on top of it like a tower and allows no more than a narrow cone of family resemblance.

6 I learned about communication by twisting my legs around yours as, in spinning a thought, we twist fiber on fiber. The strength of language does not reside in the fact that some one desire runs its whole length, but in the overlapping of many generations. Relationships form before they are written down just as grass bends before the wind, and now it is impossible to know which of us went toward the other, naked, unsteady, but, once lit, the unprepared fused with its afterimage like twenty stories of glass and steel on fire. Our lord of the mirror. I closed my eyes, afraid to resemble.

7 Is it possible to know where a word ends and my use of it begins? Or to locate the ledge of your promises to lean my head on? Even if I built a boundary out of five pounds of definition, it could not be called the shock of a wall. Nor the pain that follows. Dusk cast the houses in shadow, flattening their projections. Blurred edges, like memory or soul, an event you turn away from. Yet I also believe that a sharp picture is not always preferable. Even when people come in pairs, their private odds should be made the most of. You went in search of more restful altitudes, of ideally clear language. But the bridge that spans the mind-body gap enjoys gazing downstream. All this time I was holding my umbrella open.

8 I wondered if it was enough to reverse subject and object, or does it matter if the bow moves up or down the string. Blind possibility, say hunger, thickened. How high the sea of language runs. Its white sails, sexual, inviting to apply the picture, or black, mourning decline in navigation. I know, but cannot say, what a violin sounds like. Driftwood migrates toward the margin, the words gather momentum, wash back over their own sheets of insomnia. No harbor. No haul of silence.

CURVES TO THE APPLE

9 There were no chronicles. The dimensions of emptiness instead of heroic feats. This was taken as proof that female means lack. As if my body were only layers on layers of windowpane. The whole idea of depth smells fishy. But there are thicker transparencies where the sentence goes wrong as soon as you do something, because doing carries its own negative right into the center of the sun and blots out the metonymies of desire. In this neck of the womb. Later, sure enough, the applications fall away even if we cling to the exaggerated fireworks of lost purpose.

10 It is best to stop as soon as you hear a word in a language you don't know. Its opaqueness stands, not as a signpost to the adventures of misunderstanding, but a wall where touch goes deaf, and without explanations hanging in the air, waiting to be supported by the clotheslines of childhood. As I looked up, a boy approached me and offered to carry my bag because it was raining. Wet laundry flapped in the wind.

11 Heavy with soot, the rain drummed on the tin roof of the garage, eager to fall into language and be solved in the manner of mysteries. I tried to hear the line between the drumming and the duller thud on the street, like the phantom beat between two rhythms. An umbrella would have complicated the score. No gift of the singular: the sounds merged with traffic noise too gray to make a difference between woman and mother, or grammar and theology. Not like the children playing tag, throwing their slight weight into flight from the ever changing "it." Though the drops hit my face more gently than an investigating eye, the degree of slippage

12 Visibility was poor. The field limited by grammatical rules, the foghorns of language. On the sidewalk, people waiting for the bus looked out from under umbrellas and hoods, their eyes curtained by crosshatched rain, lids close to one another as when approaching sleep or pain. An adherence to darkness that refuses exact praise like reaching for a glass. Even when I had emptied mine, I had not gotten to the bottom of the things in plain view. A play of reflections and peculiar. The drops of water traveled diagonally across the paradigms as the bus moved on.

13 Because we cannot penetrate the soul, at most touch its outer lips with the reflected light of metaphor, the soul cannot know itself, but the dimmer light holds off loud breathing. It's not that our sense impressions lie, but that we understand their language. All through the linear seasons, the sun leaned on the shoulder of the road. Flocks of swallows lost vaster reasons to the sky. Salt travel. Statues which adorn the unconscious. My hopes crushed by knowledge of anatomy. Or is this another error, this theory of erosion, of all we cannot see?

14 On the fourth day, I took the rain in my mouth, and the fish sank deeper, lighting up in glints like time passing. The bus moved off, a long sliding door. Behind it, the row of houses suddenly larger, a mass of stone and wood to constrict your chest, as when you take a wrong turn to the side of your head which is dark with war and strangling and then are weak from loss of blood, a fishline wound around your neck. The dark was an obstacle. It would shortly come between me and the street, but its name made me want to touch its velvet beginning. Even though I've known complete rejection, words will still send me in pursuit of chimeras.

15 The room inside me has disappeared. At night, when all is quiet, I no longer hear the pictures shifting on the walls when I walk fast. Only the pump in the basement. I wonder whether the space has folded in on itself like a tautology, or been colonized. You think the wine has washed it out, and it's true that the mirror tilted at a reckless angle. I still have the floorplan with measurements, but now that nothing corresponds to it I can only take it as part of the emptiness I try to cover up with writing. To know by my blind spot. I have always wanted to dilate my landscape for the piano and the long labor of losing the self. Though I'm too nearsighted for clouds. If I had lived a different image.

16 If I were a mother I would naturally possess the pure crystalline logic which is the prerequisite and found in most well-appointed duals. Only, it is hard not to slip on the ice because there is no friction. Back to rougher sentences, I said, to the incomplete self and choice of desires. This postulated the vacancy as social rather than biological, and that it need not be filled. My body was calm, even naked, safe in its transparency.

17 This is where grammatical terror opens a distance between you and yourself in order to insert the mirror. And where you had hoped it would be a serene blue surface reflecting the flight of a bird or fancy, the waves rise up against each other and crash, strangling, screaming. What has become of logic? You know enough to skip explanation and displace your own weight in water. You hope the motion will wear itself out, its speed braked by words. History has taught you that all desires want to do away with themselves.

18 As long as I wanted to be a man I considered thought as a keen blade cutting through the uncertain brambles in my path. Later, I let it rust under the stairs. The image was useless, given the nature of my quest. Each day, I draw the distance to cover out of an anxiety as deep as the roots of language. I keep my eye on the compass while engaging the whole width of the field, and whereas, to others, I may look like a blur of speed from one point in time to another, I know I am not advancing an inch and will never arrive. Even if I could arrive the mirror would only show the other mirrors I have set up at every stop to catch the spirit of passage.

19 I worried about the previous occupants of the house, their traces burned off by daylight, unless a silence that grows more attentive as the hours wear on, some intangible bond among absent faces that outweighs my lack of purpose, the stillness of my posture. This is what makes the wallpaper so neutral as far as my affection goes. Its pattern rotates bits of landscape into orbits of definitive distance, like chrysanthemums celebrating All Souls'. It's not one of those pictures which I cannot get outside of because my language repeats it to me over and over, inexorably. From behind rocks, a boat is heading into a promise of archipelagos and coral islands, then travels into more faded patches as into so much fog.

20 With difficulty, the lamp outlined the limits of the dark where the objects sat so opaque, so at home in their silence. Not a clarity in which all likeness disappears, not breaking into space like a triumphant bird. Rather a dim lamp. Specks of dust moving in its cone, a fine attachment to light against the grain. As you might be stirred beyond all reason by the signs that form a word, easy motion, unbuttoned coincidence, clearing lips in a euphoria skidding toward the urban periphery. Or again, lost in the fog. It will cling to you no matter how heavy your boots.

21 The dusk swelled and lengthened every shadow, a version of time not suited to the ephemeral. For if you concern yourself with what belongs, but doesn't fit, turning your wrist like an angler out of season who, sure of his catch, throws his line into a cross section of air, the picture forces its particular application on you. Schools of thought emerge and are hooked in an instant. Others flit across the danger zone with tail fins flashing, and the alphabet ceases to be a disposition of the mind. I wondered, would a bracelet strengthen my analytical capacity.

22 As long as we can see the facts, you said, your eye frantic for touch, not a body of water which is beautiful in itself, but still a source of satisfaction in the stress of the air. So I tried to get the fact of rain down on the paper, the way it appeases the green, the haze rising too subtly to make me believe in an unbroken circle. It seeped away, into the pores, watering landscapes as removed from the pressure of perception as the nature of between, though the traces of ink looked a little like the shadows of clouds written on the ground. But any body being penetrated, all that is looked at.

23 Given the distance of communication, I hope the words aren't idling on the map on my fingertips, but igniting wild acres within the probabilities of spelling. As a hawk describes circles whose inner emptiness bespeaks the power of gravity, where the lever catches on a cog of the world. There, the mild foreground for buying bread, for the averted doubt that the hand will encounter. There, with dizzy attention, I hold the because, another key to the bewitchment of words.

24 In the middle of rainy weather, sleep was pinning me down on the bed, lids barnacled shut with adjectives in color. Sleep, which cannot be divided from itself or into parts of speech, pushing a whole sea at my body so unable to swallow its grandiose and monotonous splendor. The air already slowing to the crucial stillness of noon. Would there ever again be ground for walking? I mean, the field of understanding does not extend to lying down. Later, writing would articulate the absence of voice, pictures, the absence of objects, clothes, the absence of body.

25 Never mind wholeness. Though it worries me that I have no sense of it. How can I approach the task without all of me gathered in one fist like, if I were a man I'd say, a stone I want to hurl or, as I'm not, an entire tune cradled on its fulcrum. Then I could be sure I won't get stuck if I try to sing. But I get stuck. Single notes occupy my voice with their vertical shadows, luminous blue, so long, so stretched, so content to sink slowly back into. Or a flock of swallows, alarmed suddenly, sucked crazily in all directions. The light appropriates, even to the unsounded spasms of treble and flight, and the fields stretch into what, lacking male parameters, must be nowhere.

26 It rained so much that I began to confuse puddles with the life of the mind. Perhaps what I had taken for reflection was only soaking up the world, a cross of sponge and good will through the center of the eye. But to describe the inner world, you know, by definition, even the patient definitions of psychology, is impossible. Hard to know if it can be lived. Revoked edge of water and dry land. A falling fear. The sudden color of a word. But it's the sky, pale gray, abundantly thrown back from far enough behind the eye, as you imagine an image, seeing earth in every direction.

27 The labyrinth of language. You know your way as you go in one bony side, but out the other you're lost in spiral frequencies, unsettled air as coiled as who'll believe it. Not for the first time has a wave broken on a hammer, anvil, or suddenly, which is a deep space where sentences breathe differently and the rider rocks in the stirrup. Caress of hair like dark approaching a naked voice. Or scales. If the air won't take my word I can't trace half a circle, falling, dizzy, into the confusion of canals.

28 If I promise day after day: tomorrow I'll come to see you, am I saying the same thing every day, or does a rainbow grow frenetic in the to and fro between eye and image, bits of light torn from a mirage which doesn't appease desire, but only fits into its own shape? Incestuous words, reflecting reference as mere decor or possibly a blanket. Orphaned so severely, the eye still trusts that emptiness is ready to receive the rain.

29 Once the word "pain" has replaced crying, behavior functions as landscape, and the philosopher can treat a question like an illness. The decisive moment is now, but dust has no particular object as it rises to the occasion, and only when I blink can I still see the distant shore. Nothing had prepared me for the end of monotony. I've always admired thin lines like the string of the marionette, which replaces consciousness catching in the hollow of the knee. But alone on a page. Or crossed out.

30 Look at that blue, you said, detaching the color from the sky as if it were a membrane. A mutilation you constantly sharpen your language for. I had wanted to begin slowly because, whether in the direction of silence or things have a way of happening, you must not watch as the devil picks your shadow off the ground. Nor the scar lines on your body. Raw sky. If everybody said, I know what pain is, could we not set clocks by the violent weather sweeping down from the north? Lesions of language. The strained conditions of colored ink. Or perhaps it is a misunderstanding to peel back skin in order to bare the mechanics of the mirage.

LAWN OF
EXCLUDED MIDDLE

for Claude Royet-Journoud

■ ■ ■ ■ ■ ■

PART ONE

LAWN OF EXCLUDED MIDDLE

I When I say I believe that women have a soul and that its substance contains two carbon rings the picture in the foreground makes it difficult to find its application back where the corridors get lost in ritual sacrifice and hidden bleeding. But the four points of the compass are equal on the lawn of the excluded middle where full maturity of meaning takes time the way you eat a fish, morsel by morsel, off the bone. Something that can be held in the mouth, deeply, like darkness by someone blind or the empty space I place at the center of each poem to allow penetration.

2 I'm looking out the window at other windows. Though the pane masquerades as transparent I know it is impenetrable just as too great a show of frankness gives you a mere paper draft on revelations. As if words were passports, or arrows that point to the application we might make of them without considering the difference of biography and life. Still, depth of field allows the mind to drift beyond its negative pole to sun catching on a maple leaf already red in August, already thinner, more translucent, preparing to strip off all that separates it from its smooth skeleton. Beautiful, flamboyant phrase that trails off without predicate, intending disappearance by approaching it, a toss in the air.

3 I put a ruler in my handbag, having heard men talk about their sex. Now we have correct measurement and a stickiness between collar and neck. It is one thing to insert yourself into a mirror, but quite another to get your image out again and have your errors pass for objectivity. Vitreous. As in humor. A change in perspective is caused by the ciliary muscle, but need not be conciliatory. Still, the eye is a camera, room for everything that is to enter, like the cylinder called the satisfaction of hollow space. Only language grows such grass-green grass.

4 Even if a woman sits at a loom, it does not mean she must weave a cosmogony or clothes to cover the emptiness underneath. It might just be a piece of cloth which, like any center of attention, absorbs the available light the way a waterfall can form a curtain of solid noise through which only time can pass. She has been taught to imagine other things, but does not explain, disdaining defense while her consciousness streams down the rapids. The light converges on what might be the hollow of desire or the incomplete self, or just lint in her pocket. Her hour will also come with the breaking of water.

5 Because I refuse to accept the opposition of night and day I must pit other, subtler periodicities against the emptiness of being an adult. Their traces inside my body attempt precariously, like any sign, to produce understanding, but though nothing may come of that, the grass is growing. Can words play my parts and also find their own way to the house next door as rays converge and solve their differences? Or do notes follow because drawn to a conclusion? If we don't signal our love, reason will eat our heart out before it can admit its form of mere intention, and we won't know what has departed.

6 All roads lead, but how does a sentence do it? Nothing seems hidden, but it goes by so fast when I should like to see it laid open to view whether the engine resembles combustion so that form becomes its own explanation. We've been taught to apply solar principles, but must find on our own where to look for Rome the way words rally to the blanks between them and thus augment the volume of their resonance.

7 It's a tall order that expects pain to crystallize into beauty. And we must close our eyes to conceive of heaven. The inside of the lid is fertile in images unprovoked by experience, or perhaps its pressure on the eyeball equals prayer in the same way that inference is a transition toward assertion, even observing rites of dawn against a dark and empty background. I have read that female prisoners to be hanged must wear rubber pants and a dress sewn shut around the knees because uterus and ovaries spill with the shock down the shaft.

8 The meaning of certainty is getting burned. Though truth will still escape us, we must put our hands on bodies. Staying safe is a different death, the instruments of defense eating inward without evening out the score. As the desire to explore my body's labyrinth did, leading straight to the center of nothing. From which projected my daily world of representation with bright fictional fireworks. Had I overinvested in spectacle? In mere fluctuations of light which, like a bird's wingbeat, must with time slow to the point of vanishing? What about buying bread or singing in the dark? Even if the ground for our assumptions is the umber of burnt childhood we're driven toward the sun as if logic had no other exit.

9 Though the way I see you depends on I don't know how many codes I have absorbed unawares, like germs or radiation, I am certain the conflicting possibilities of logic and chemistry have contaminated the space between us. Emptiness is imperative for feeling to take on substance, for its vibrations to grow tangible, a faintly trembling beam that supports the whole edifice. Caught between the thickness of desire and chill clarity, depth dissolved its contours with intemperate movements inside the body where much can be gathered. Can I not say a cry, a laugh are full of meaning, a denseness for which I have no words that would not channel its force into shallower waters, mere echo of oracles?

10 My anxiety made you wary. As if I tried to draw you into a new kind of sexuality, a flutter of inner emptiness implying hunger to frame the momentary flight of birds with emotional reference and heat. Any initiation anticipates absolute abandon with the body misunderstood as solid, whereas images dissolve their objects. Even with deep water ahead, even though the shores of syllogism may be flooded, we must not turn around. Behind us, incursions into our own field of vision, a mirror to lose our body out of the corner of an eye. It may look like a sentence we understand, yet quenches no thirst, no matter how hard we stroke it. But anxiety is a password which does not require a special tone of voice. Rather than to immersion in mysteries I was only leading you to common ground.

11 Whenever you're surprised that I should speak your language I am suddenly wearing too many necklaces and breasts, even though feeling does not produce what is felt, and the object of observation is something else again. Not modulating keys, not the splash that makes us take to another element, just my body alarmingly tangible, like furniture that exceeds its function, a shape I cannot get around. The way one suddenly knows the boulder in the road for a boulder, immovable, as if not always there, unmodified by inner hollows or the stray weeds and their dusty green, a solid obstacle with only trompe-l'oeil exits toward the subtler body of light accumulating in the distance.

12 I worried about the gap between expression and intent, afraid the world might see a fluorescent advertisement where I meant to show a face. Sincerity is no help once we admit to the lies we tell on nocturnal occasions, even in the solitude of our own heart, wishcraft slanting the naked figure from need to seduce to fear of possession. Far better to cultivate the gap itself with its high grass for privacy and reference gone astray. Never mind that it is not philosophy, but raw electrons jumping from orbit to orbit to ready the pit for the orchestra, scrap meanings amplifying the succession of green perspectives, moist fissures, spasms on the lips.

CURVES TO THE APPLE

13 Words too can be wrung from us like a cry from that space which doesn't seem to be the body nor a metaphor curving into perspective. Rather the thickness silence gains when pressed. The ghosts of grammar veer toward shape while my hopes still lie embedded in a quiet myopia from which they don't want to arise. The mistake is to look for explanations where we should just watch the slow fuse burning. Nerve of confession. What we let go we let go.

14 Because we use the negative as if no explanation were needed the void we cater to is, like anorexia, a ferment of hallucinations. Here, the bird's body equals the rhythm of wingbeats which, frantic, disturb their own lack of origin, fear of falling, indigenous gray. Static electricity. Strobe map. Gap gardening. The sun feeds on its dark core for a set of glistening blood, in a space we can't fathom except as pollution colors it.

15 The word "not" seems like a poor expedient to designate all that escapes my understanding like the extra space between us when I press my body against yours, perhaps the distance of desire, which we carry like a skyline and which never allows us to be where we are, as if past and future had their place whereas the present dips and disappears under your feet, so suddenly your stomach is squeezed up into your throat as the plane crashes. This is why some try to stretch their shadow across the gap as future fame while the rest of us take up residence in the falling away of land, even though our nature is closer to water.

16 The affirmation of the double negative tempts us to invent a myth of meaning where the light loops its wavelength through dark hollows into unheard-of Americas, or a double-tongued flute speeds decimals over the whole acoustic range of the landscape till it exhausts itself with excess of effect brought home. Can I walk in your sleep, in order to defer obedience and assent to my own waking? Or will the weight of error pull me down below the symmetries of the round world? Touching bottom means the water's over your head. And you can't annul a shake of that by shaking it again.

17 In Providence, you can encounter extinct species, an equestrian statue, say, left hoof raised in progress toward the memory of tourists. Caught in its career of immobility, but with surface intact, waiting to prove that it can resist the attack of eyes even though dampened by real weather, even though historical atmosphere is mixed with exhaust like etymology with the use of a word or bone with sentence structure. No wonder we find it difficult to know our way about and tend to stay indoors.

18 A window can draw you into the distance within proximity all the way to where it vanishes with the point. This is not a hocuspocus which can be performed only by kinship terms. The glass seems to secure perspectives that can shoulder the cold stare of so many third persons while our image is resolved in favor of inaccessible riverbeds. Alternating small and large measures, the dust on the pane is part of the attraction, a way of allowing the environment in. So would a stone's throw, substituting the high frequencies of shattering for the play of reflections.

19 We know that swallows are drawn to window panes, etching swift lurching streaks across and sometimes crashing. I picked up the body as if easing the vast sky through a narrow pulse toppling over itself. Caught between simulacrum and paradox, the hard air. Even if a body could survive entering its own image, the mirror is left empty, no fault in the glass breaking the evenness of light.

20 What's left over if I subtract the fact that my leg goes up from the fact that I raise it? A link to free will or never trying as only our body knows to disobey an even trade to the sound of a fiddle. Something tells me not to ask this question and accept the movement. The speed of desire like a hot wind sweeping the grass or flash of water under the bridge. For doing itself seems not to have any volume: an extensionless point, the point of a needle out to draw blood regardless.

21 This is not thinking, you said, more what colors it, like a smell entering our breath even to the seat of faith under the left nipple. Like the children I could have borne shaping my body toward submission and subterfuge. It is possible, I admitted, to do physics in inches as well as in centimeters, but a concept is more than a convenience. It takes us through earnest doorways to always the same kind of example. No chance of denser vegetation, of the cool shadow of firs extending this line of reasoning into the dark.

22 My love was deep and therefore lasted only the space of one second, unable to expand in more than one dimension at a time. The same way deeper meaning may constrict a sentence right out of the language into an uneasiness with lakes and ponds. In language nothing is hidden or our own, its light indifferent to holes in the present or postulates beginning with ourselves. Still, you may travel alone and yet be accompanied by my good wishes.

23 Look in thy heart and write, you quoted. As if we could derive the object from desire, or proper breathing from the structure of transitivity. It's true, the brain is desperate for an available emptiness to house its clutter, as a tone can only grow from a space of silence, lifted by inaudible echoes as birds are by the air inside their bones. So we reach down, although it cannot save us, to the hollows inside the body, to extend them into so many journeys into the world, so many words shelling the echo of absence onto the dry land.

24 In the way well-being contains the possibility of pain a young boy may show the meekness we associate with girls, or an excess of sperm, on occasion, come close to spirituality. But a name is an itch to let the picture take root inside its contour though sentences keep shifting like sand, and a red patch may be there or not. All heights are fearful. We must cast arbitrary nets over the unknown, knot the earth's rim to the sky with a rope of orisons. For safety. For once human always an acrobat.

25 Meaning is like going up to someone I would be with, though often the distance doesn't seem to lessen no matter how straight my course. Busy moving ahead, I can't also observe myself moving, let alone assess the speed of full steam minus fiction and sidetracked in metric crevices. It's hard to identify with the image of an arrow even if it points only to the application we make of it. But then, meandering does not guarantee thought either, though it simulates its course toward wider angles, which make us later than we are, our fingers the space of already rust from the key. Even the weight of things can no longer measure our calculations. Conquered by our own scope we offer no resistance to the blue transparency, the startling downpour of sun.

26 I wanted to settle down on a surface, a map perhaps, where my near-sightedness might help me see the facts. But grammar is deep. Even though it only describes, it submerges the mind in a maelstrom without discernable bottom, the dimensions of possibles swirling over the fixed edge of nothingness. Like looking into blue eyes all the way through to the blue sky without even a cloudbank or flock of birds to cling to. What are we searching behind the words as if a body of information could not also bruise? It is the skeleton that holds on longest to its native land.

27 For a red curve to be a smile it needs a face around it, company of its kind to capture our attention by the between, the bait of difference and constant of desire. Then color sweeping over cheeks is both expansion of internal transport and an airing of emotion. Understanding, too, enters more easily through a gap between than where a line is closed upon itself. This is why comparisons, for all their limping, go farther even than the distance of beauty, rose or fingered dawn, or of remembering contracts signed in blood.

28 Electric seasons. Night has become as improbable as a sea forever at high tide. The sheer excess of light makes for a lack of depth, denying our fall from grace, the way a membrane is all surface. Or the way we, clamoring for sense, exclude so many unions of words from the sphere of language. As if one could fall off the edge of the earth. Why do we fear the dark as unavoidable defeat when it alone is constant, and we'd starve if it stopped watering the lawn of dreams.

29 You were determined to get rid of your soul by expressing it completely, rubbing the silver off the mirror in hope of a new innocence of body on the other side of knowing. A limpid zone which would not wholly depend on our grammar in the way the sea draws its color from the sky. Noon light, harsh, without shadow. Each gesture intending only its involvement with gravity, a pure figure of reach, as the hyperbola is for its asymptotes or circles widening on the water for the stone that broke the surface. But the emigration is rallied, reflections regather across the ripples. Everything in our universe curves back to the apple.

30 The capacity to move my hand from left to right arises on a margin of indecision and doubt winding into vertiginous inner stairwells, but only when adjacent shadows have cooled the long summer sun toward a more introverted, solitary quality of light for the benefit of eyes tensing to see the dark before concepts. This is an attempt to make up for inner emptiness in the way that Fred Astaire and Ginger Rogers dance with more desperate brio to add a third dimension to their characters. Nevertheless the capacity does not explain how the meaning of individual words can make a tent over a whole argument. It is not a feeling, but a circular movement to represent the transfer of visibility toward dream without abrogating the claims of body.

31 As if I had to navigate both forward and backward, part of me turned away from where I'm going, taking the distance of long corridors to allow for delay and trouble, for keeping in the dark while being led on. In this way Chinese characters seem to offer their secret without revealing it, invitation to enter a labyrinth which, like that of the heart, may not have a center. It is replaced by being lost which I don't like to dwell on because the search for motivation can only drive us downward toward potential that is frightening in proportion to its depth and sluicegates to disappearance. It is much better, I have been advised, just to drift with the stream. The ink washes into a deeper language, and in the end the water runs clear.

■ ■ ■ ■ ■ ■

PART TWO

THE PERPLEXING HABIT OF FALLING

I ▪ THE ATTRACTION OF THE GROUND

In the beginning there were torrential rains, and the world dissolved in puddles, even though we were well into the nuclear age and speedier methods. Constant precipitation drenched the dry point of the present till it leaked a wash of color all the way up to the roots of our hair. I wanted to see mysteries at the bottom of the puddles, but they turned out to be reflections that made our heads swim. The way a statue's eyes bring our stock of blindness to the surface. Every thought swelled to the softness of flesh after a long bath, the lack of definition essential for happiness, just as not knowing yourself guarantees a life of long luke-warm days stretching beyond the shadow of pure reason on the side-walk. All this was common practice. Downpour of sun. Flood of young leafiness. A slight unease caused by sheer fill of body. Running over and over like the light spilled westward across the continent, a river we couldn't cross without our moment, barely born, drowning in its own translucent metaphor.

The silence, which matted my hair like a room with the windows shut too long, filled with your breath. As if you didn't need the weight of words in your lungs to keep your body from dispersing like so many molecules over an empty field. Being a woman and without history, I wanted to explore how the grain of the world runs, hoping for backward and forward the way sentences breathe even this side of explanation. But you claimed that words absorb all perspective and blot out the view just as certain parts of the body obscure others on the curve of desire. Or again, as the message gets lost in the long run, while we still see the messenger panting, unflagging, through the centuries. I had thought it went the other way round and was surprised as he came out of my mouth in his toga, without even a raincoat. I had to lean far out the window to follow his now unencumbered course, speeding your theory toward a horizon flat and true as a spirit level.

My legs were so interlaced with yours I began to think I could never use them on my own again. Not even if I shaved them. As if emotion had always to be a handicap. But maybe the knots were a picture of my faint unrest at having everything and not more, like wind caught in the trees with no open space to get lost, a tension toward song hanging in the air like an unfinished birdcry, or the smell of the word verbena, or apples that would not succumb to the attraction of the ground. In a neutral grammar love may be a refrain screamed through the loud-speakers, a calibration of parallels or bone structure strong enough to support verisimilitude. A FOR SALE sign in red urged us to participate in our society, while a whole flock of gulls stood in the mud by the river, ready to extend the sky with their wings. Another picture. Is it called love or nerves, you said, when everything is on the verge of happening? But I was unable to distinguish between waves and corpuscles because I had rings under my eyes, and appearances are fragile. Though we already live partly underground it must be possible to find a light that is exacting and yet allows us to be ourselves even while taking our measure.

Although you are thin you always seemed to be in front of my eyes, putting back in the body the roads my thoughts might have taken. As if forward and backward meant no more than right and left, and the earth could just as easily reverse its spin. So that we made each other the present of a stage where time would not pass, and only space would age, encompassing all 200,000 dramatic situations, but over the rest of the proceedings, the increase of entropy and unemployment. Meanwhile we juggled details of our feelings into an exaggeration which took the place of explanation and consequences remained in the kind of repose that, like a dancer's, already holds the leap toward inside turning out.

Your arms were embracing like a climate that does not require being native. They held me responsive, but I still wondered about the other lives I might have lived, the unused cast of characters stored within me, outcasts of actuality no stranger than my previous selves. As if a word should be counted a lie for all it misses. I could imagine my body arching up toward other men in a high-strung vertigo that scored a virtual accompaniment to our real dance, deep phantom chords echoing from nowhere though with the force of long acceleration, of flying home from a lost wedding. Stakes and mistakes. Big with sky, with bracing cold, with the drone of aircraft, the measures of distance hang in the air before falling in thick drops. The child will be pale and thin. Though it had infiltrated my bones, the thought was without marrow. More a feeling that might accompany a thought, a ply of consonants, an outward motion of the eye.

I began to long for respite from attention, the freedom of interruption. The clouds of feeling inside my head, though full of soft light, needed a breeze or the pull of gravity. More rain. As if I suddenly couldn't speak without first licking my lips, spelling my name, enumerating the days of the week. Would separation act as an astringent? Ink our characters more sharply? I tried to push the idea aside, afraid of losing the dimensions of nakedness, but it kept turning up underfoot, tripping me. Clearly, the journey would mean growing older, flat tiredness, desire out of tune. Much practice is needed for two-dimensional representation whether in drawing or rooms, and it emaciates our undertakings in the way that lack of sleep narrows thinking to a point without echoes, the neck of the hourglass. You may be able to travel fast forward without looking back, but I paint my lashes to slow the child in my face and climb the winding stairs back to a logic whose gaps are filled by mermaids.

Many questions were left in the clearing we built our shared life in. Later sheer size left no room for imagining myself standing outside it, on the edge of an empty day. I knew I didn't want to part from this whole which could be said to carry its foundation as much as resting on it, just as a family tree grows downward, its branches confounding gravitation and gravidity. I wanted to continue lying alongside you, two parallel, comparable lengths of feeling, and let the stresses of the structure push our sleep to momentum and fullness. Still, a fallow evening stretches into unknown elsewheres, seductive with possibility, doors open onto a chaos of culs-de-sac, of could-be, of galloping off on the horse in the picture. And whereto? A crowning mirage or a question like What is love? And where? Does it enter with a squeeze, or without, bringing, like interpretation, its own space from some other dimension? Or is it like a dream corridor forever extending its concept toward extreme emptiness, like that of atoms?

Is it because we cannot capture our own selves or because logically nothing is on its own that we turn to each other for reflection and echo as philosophers always go back to the same props and propositions? If you return from far enough away you perhaps never left, but it still takes coats off, or character, to warp the arrow. A circle is a figure almost as clear as a straight line, but covers more territory, even water, the way the relation of two people is not bound to follow rules on separable prefixes. We knew the state of our affairs and pooled them. Once your reflection surfaced out of deep water, the fragile mirror prohibiting the turbulence of touch, I wondered if I would not trade this transparency for a white space of its own without allusions, provided the ice was solid enough to walk across. Even though it was summer, we moved rather like snow blown by the wind, not easy to make tracks on, melting and refreezing in harsh ridges.

What once had been vehemence now seemed to inhibit us. We could never again come up to its watermark, with all the ambivalence in the air. You seemed instead like too thin skin, shrinking suspiciously from close-ups, unaware that I was also on my guard, ready to retreat as soon as the mind gets soft with the warmth and begins to shed its clothes. Once you blur the distinction between equal and equivocal, space is interrupted and disappears in subcutaneous shivers. But it would be a pity if nothing more happened between us because we have memorized ourselves too thoroughly and are wary even as we travel through the passes and impasses of sleep, through layers of velvet density, back to the innermost desire anchored in all our questions and actions, anchored so deeply that we cannot touch it.

To test if I could see your child as my own without preparatory pregnancy or periods of nausea to allow for resistance, I began to take walks in the dark. "Seeing as" is not part of perception. And for that reason like seeing and again not like. In the hot summer night, perspective might be conceived to travel both forward and backward to the same point of vanishing time, a conception after the fact, a gestation backward into the stability of impossible desires that might draw him as the sea does if you look too long at its spectacle. And he comes padding at night on bare feet and takes a long look at my body before whimpering to you of fear of the dark, so that you'll draw the sheet up and protect him against the shock of female nakedness.

Dynasties of space seem to claim him, this child who embraces his vertigo though atoms as porous as the solar system make images vanish into intervals, and intervals into sheer emptiness. His leaps delirious, body flung from mountain tops in pursuit of a remote self, so hard to trap in the subtlest net of language, games, or set of mirrors. Though the temperature may fall there's not a doubt in his green blood that he can always squeeze a cushion from the air, a wealth of longest tracks setting him gently down in his picture of the world. No measurements disturb the chances of fun and blame or spring's exorbitant unfolding in his veins. Anxiety comes later with a disproportion of raincoats and knowing the groundlessness of our beliefs. I've lost my skin to immense, complex summers and the meaning of words to the uncertainty of fact. Not just the rivers, the riverbeds too are shifting.

The injury was in not responding until the shiniest sheet of tension lay glistening between us and the balance of power started to slip on the ice. At the speed of slight the clocks run counter. I tried to recall the moment when I realized that wind losing momentum may not mean holes in the argument or ice so that the fish can breathe. We needn't quarrel if, instead of surveying our relation from within, we allowed that we had each drawn the line with flying colors, so that you saw red zigzag lightning where I lay down on a green lawn. Moving at different speeds we contracted different diseases and took the most negative measure of each other's hunger. This was why the ratio of emotional to body heat remained impaired even though we wore boots and heavy coats. It would take wrapping up in words.

You were busy planting your picture of the world into your child's mind. Mine, in comparison, seemed more like the hotel slated for demolition, beyond redecorating. From the window, not the expected distance of beauty, but a row of scraggy young trees facing a church covered from top to bottom with scaffolding which allowed only rare glimpses of white volutes and projections. One of the trees seemed scraggier than the rest, perhaps blighted, but on the whole it was two lines of wood at different stages, and I was learning to read between them as slowly as possible. A hitch in time. The way a look into a mirror saves miles. If the scaffolding cast its shadow over your boy, who was running circles around its posts, he remained unaware, his skin hardly darkened. He expects definitions on the order of freeways and runaway nebulae, not horizons contracting to flywheel and cog, hard fiber in the pit of the stomach.

I worked hard at keeping perspective in the family and periodically faced in your direction as the faithful toward the East. Your space was framed so differently from mine that it located your "here" around the curve of the horizon, unreachable by even my longest sentence. All I could see was a glare as over the Great Fire of London. So that landscape became a religion of surface, teaching divine imperfection and replacing baptism by fire. You thought it was improbable that the concept of original sin was upset by electricity in motion any more than by gravity's competing for the apple. The question of intimacy did not come up to the temperature, but had to be raised so we could get out of the building already full of smoke. It may be easier to speed the process of oxidation than to hold on to the illusions of communication. Nor can the sign for water quench the flames in my lungs. It only inhales loads of silence which connect and separate according to the twists and turns of the plot.

Later, my shadow stopped following and, after a moment of holding its breath, steadily lengthened my progress ahead of me, obscuring other roads as if only a narrow consistency could inherit a goal. It was also at this time that the mirror began to show the back of my head, and my stare would speed its moving on while I stood still as a cat within her fur. Even so, we know the way to go is outward and stretch pale roots toward the world, of which we really know nothing. The same way we walk on credit, swinging the body forward, confident that, though for one moment in each step we tread the void, it won't close over our head. You, the more courageous, had even put forth a child with ruthless appetites and so bridged wider intervals toward those edges of experience where impressions seem sharp as line drawings just before they drop into the virtual and vicarious, mysteries beyond the vested interests of before and because.

Even at your nakedest, your nakedness would not reach all the way to your face, the way a rock by the sea is always veiled in water and foam as in a memory of deep space. Or perhaps I was looking for something beyond my capacity of seeing, and the shifts of hiddenness were only in the image I carried somewhere between head and dark of stomach as I searched the woods for poisonous mushrooms. The technique is to knock them out with a stick and tread them to pulp, which saves lives and provides entertainment. Actually I prefer stories with sharp edges cut by blades manufactured with great precision in Solingen, Germany. These I use like a religion to keep me on the straight and narrative which, like computers and gods, admits only yes or no. No straying into ambiguous underbrush where hidden desire is not made any clearer by intermittent fulfillment, the light and shadow playing over my rush of wildwater actions while I feel I'm sitting motionless on the bank.

With the body running down inexorably, how can we each day reweave our net of closeness and distance? But though time burns at both ends, it rolls around the clock, and evening replays events of the day in a new light, showing perhaps electric waves instead of raindrops glittering on a spiderweb. The relation is not resemblance, but pulling the trigger on a nerve. While time takes the shortest cut right into consciousness, physical cause stops at the door. There remains an ultimate gap, as between two people, that not even a penis can bridge, a point at which we lose sight of the erection crossing a horizon in the mind. This is accompanied by slight giddiness as when we jump over our shadow or admire the waves rolling incomprehensible resolutions in a border of darker and darker gray. It dispenses us from trying to draw profit from attention to ritual, like watching the spider ride its memory from periphery to center orb at nightfall.

You went through the school of velocity hoping for a speed worthy of flight where you would feel stillness in your bones while falling into deep thought. Not a space I could thrust my breasts into while maintaining the mountain climber's three points of contact with the surface, using the fourth to goad time toward climax. The height of a mountain does not depend on how we climb it or equality of chance. Steep territory. Face to rock-face. Different scales of gravity code a slow body against dreams of flying, both menaced by the thin complexities of the air. The problem was less securing a foothold than an echo off the cliff. What I am doing here is hanging a name on a difficulty, a common alternative to the sheer effort toward telling ground. The turtle is geologically the oldest of our extant amphibia. Even though we live on a decently slow-moving planet, I sometimes think the world might be edging away and out of reach.

I badly wanted a story of my own. As if there were proof in spelling. But what if my experience were the kind of snow that does not accumulate? A piling of instants that did not amount to a dimension? What if wandering within my own limits I came back naked, with features too faint for the mirror, unequal to the demands of the night? In the long run I could not deceive appearances: Days and nights were added without adding up. Nothing to recount in bed before falling asleep. Even memory was not usable, a landscape hillocky with gravitation but without monuments, it did not hold the eye, did not hinder its glide toward the horizon where the prose of the world gives way to the smooth functioning of fear. If the wheel so barely touches the ground the speed must be enormous.

The concept of an inner picture is misleading. Like those on the screen, it takes the outer picture as a model, yet their uses are no more alike than statistics and bodies. Figures, we know, can proceed without any regard for reality, no matter how thin the fabric. True, the missing pieces can be glued in, but if you look for the deep you won't frighten your vertigo away. An ambition to fathom need not hold water. Stay on shore, put on more sweaters, and let the roar of the breakers swallow your urge to scream. If not the clouds themselves, their reflections withdraw with the tide. Then there is the familiar smell of wet sand and seaweed, debris of every kind, including hypodermics, condoms, oozing filth. My outer self comes running on pale legs to claim my share, while my inner picture stands dazed, blinking behind sunglasses, demanding a past that might redeem the present.

I knew that true or false is irrelevant in the pursuit of knowledge which must find its own ways to avoid falling as it moves toward horizons of light. We can't hope to prove gravity from the fact that it tallies with the fall of an apple when the nature of tallying is what Eve's bite called into question. My progress was slowed down by your hand brushing against my breast, just as travel along the optic nerve brakes the rush of light. But then light does not take place, not even in bed. It is like the kind of language that vanishes into communication, as you might into my desire for you. It takes attention focused on the fullness of shadow to give light a body that weighs on the horizon, though without denting its indifference.

I thought I could get to the bottom of things by taking my distance from logic, but only fell as far as the immediate. Here the moment flaunted its perfect roundness and could not be left behind because it accelerated with me, intense like roses blooming in the dark whereas I was still figuring out: are red roses at night darker than white ones, and all cats gray? But at some point we have to pass from explanation to description in the heroic hope that it will reach right out into experience, the groundswell flooding my whole being like heat or pollution, though the haze outside always looks as if it could easily be blown away. A cat of any color can descend into the pit behind her eyes and yawn herself right back to the bland surfaces that represent the world in the logical form we call reality. But logic is no help when you have no premises. And more and more people lacking the most modest form of them are wandering through the streets. Do we call the past perfect because it is out of sight? The present person singular is open to terrifying possibilities that strip off skin after skin till I weep as when peeling onions.

The moments of intensity did not dazzle long. Even though they took my breath into a hollow empty of time, realm back behind thought, way back behind the ceiling I stared at as a child, it was a precarious shelter breeding its own rush back to the present that moves on whether all seats are taken or not. Only in time is there space for us, and crowded at that between antecedent and consequence, and narrow, narrow. I suddenly cried. The now cast its shadow over love. Sooner or later we look out of maternal mornings at the hard sun to check income and expenditure and find the operations covert, the deficit national. There are porters on the platform, pigeons preening in the breeze showing their glassy-eyed profile. Is this a description of what I saw, a quote, a proposition relevant as a lure for feeling, or a tangle of labels and wishes, with a blind spot reserved for the old woman with shopping bags due to walk through in a few minutes? I have no answer because seeing does not so much give precise reference as imply motive, which is of no use, not even deductible when I assess the day gone by. But then it is already gone by.

Even a tree with roots square in the past cannot keep the moment from exploding in frenzy, quick bits of already gone. But there have been instants without electrical outlets, of breathing through the mouth, when I felt time pulled into a solid tightrope on which emotions swayed like acrobats and could form a foetus in the way a word casts a shadow. Then I noticed steam rising from the teapot in the picture and searched your face for another face. And found it. Open to the four winds and most stunning horoscopes. It is thanks to the flight of swallows that winter passes for the extravagance of maple leaves. An intricate reckoning of large and small cycles of light breathes deeper green in proportion to the obstruction of perspective, just as conviction may be swallowed into action, and silence be engrossed with things that baffle.

Then I realized that the world was the part of my body I could change by thinking and projected the ratio of association to sensory cortex onto the surface of the globe, inside out as you might turn a glove. Now my brain was outer space, the way we imagine it, finite but unbounded, augmenting resonance and admitting circumnavigation as idea. Now I had plantains and houses, cities, continents, planets, exclamations and concepts orbiting together, but no navel. Fear of falling gave way to a craving for salt, and oceanic feelings to persistence of frame, anticipating pictures out of great distance as when remembering a dream, or the way the white wings of a gull leave no trace, but give their rhythm to the sky. At this point you struck a match on my attention whose swerve was deflected by the heft of massive bodies. But maybe I was striking it and thinking of you as a quick leap of light, or a substance like phosphorus, the closeness of focus and hand in love consuming the last distinctions.

It takes wrestling with my whole body for words on the tip of my tongue to be found later, disembodied, on paper. A paradox easily dissolved as any use of language is a passport to the fourth dimension, which allows us to predict our future, matter of body, even rock, thinning to a reflection that I hope outlasts both the supporting mirror and the slide from sign to scissors. Meanwhile, the crossing is difficult, maybe illegal, the documents doubtful, the road through darkness, wet leaves, rotting garbage, people huddled in doorways. The vehicle breaks down, the tenor into song. Again and again, the hand on paper as if tearing the tongue from its root, translating what takes place to what takes time. This, like any fission, may cause a burst of light. A body is consumed more quickly if the temperature accelerates into love. Art takes longer, as the proverb says, but likewise shortens life. We may also get stranded, caught on the barbed wire, muscles torn and useless for the speedway.

Finally I came to prefer the risk of falling to the arrogance of solid ground and placed myself on the thin line of translation, balancing precariously between body harnessed to slowness and categories of electric charge whizzing across fields nobody could stand on. Working the charge against my retina into the cognate red of a geranium I wondered if the direction of translation should be into arithmetic or back into my native silence. Or was this a question like right or left, reversible? And could it be resolved on the nonstandard model of androgyny, sharing out the sensitive zones among the contenders? Meanwhile everyday language is using all its vigor to keep the apple in the habit of falling though the curve of the world no longer fits our flat feet and matter's become too porous to place them on.

ON LAWN OF EXCLUDED MIDDLE

1. The law of excluded middle is a venerable old law of logic. But much can be said against its claim that everything must be either true or false.

2. The idea that women cannot think logically is a not so venerable old stereotype. As an example of thinking, I don't think we need to discuss it.

3. *Lawn of Excluded Middle* plays with the idea of woman as the excluded middle. Women and, more particularly, the womb, the empty center of the woman's body, the locus of fertility.

4. This is not a syllogism.

5. This is a syllogism.

6. Poetry: an alternate, less linear logic.

7. Wittgenstein makes language with its ambiguities the ground of philosophy. His games are played on the lawn of excluded middle.

8. The picture of the world drawn by classical physics conflicts with the picture drawn by quantum theory. As A.S. Eddington says, we use classical physics on Monday, Wednesday, Friday, and quantum theory on Tuesday, Thursday, Saturday.

9. For Newton, the apple has the perplexing habit of falling. In another frame of reference, Newton is buffeted up toward the apple at rest.

10. The gravity of love encompasses ambivalence.

RELUCTANT
GRAVITIES

Two voices on a page. Or is it one? Now turning in on themselves, back into fiber and leaf, now branching into sequence, consequence, public works projects or discord. Now touching, now trapped in frames without dialog box. Both tentative, as if poring over old inscriptions, when perhaps the wall is crumbling, circuits broken, pages blown off by a fall draft.

Even if voices wrestle on the page, their impact on the air is part of their definition. In a play, for instance, the sentences would be explained by their placement on stage. We would not ask an actress what anguish her lines add up to. She would not worry what her voice touches, would let it spill over the audience, aiming beyond the folds of the curtain, at the point in the distance called the meaning of the play.

The difference of our sex, says one voice, saves us from humiliation. It makes me shiver, says the other. Your voice drops stones into feelings to sound their depth. Then warmth is truncated to war. But I'd like to fall back into simplicity as into a featherbed.

Voices, planted on the page, do not ripen or bear fruit. Here placement does not explain, but cultivates the vacancy between them. The voices pause, start over. Gap gardening which, moved inward from the right margin, suspends time. The suspension sets, is set, in type, in columns that precipitate false memories of garden, vineyard, trellis. Trembling leaf, rules of black thumb and white, invisible angle of breath and solid state.

She tries to draw a strength she dimly feels out of the weaknesses she knows, as if predicting an element in the periodic table. He wants to make a flat pebble skim across the water inside her body. He wonders if, for lack of sky, it takes on the color of skin or other cells it touches. If it rusts the bones.

The pact between page and voice is different from the compact of voice and body. The voice opens the body. Air, the cold of the air, passes through and, with a single inflection, builds large castles. The page wants proof, but bonds. The body cannot keep the voice. It spills. Foliage over the palisade.

He has put a pebble under his tongue. While her lips explode in conjectures his lisp is a new scale to practice. He wants his words to lift, against the added odds, to a truth outside him. In exchange, his father walking down the road should diminish into a symbol of age.

The page lures the voice with a promise of wood blossoming. But there is no air. No breath lives in the mouth or clouds the mirror. On stage, the body would carry the surface we call mind. Here, surface marries surface, refusing deep waters. Still, the point of encounter is here, always. Screams rise. Tears fall. Impure white, legible.

ON THE HORIZONTAL

My mother, she says, always spread, irresistibly, across the entire room, flooding me with familiarity to breed content. I feared my spongy nature and, hoping for other forms of absorption, opened the window onto more water, eyes level with its surface. And lower, till the words "I am here" lost their point with the vanishing air. Just as it's only in use that a proposition grinds its lens.

Deciphering, he says, is not a horizontal motion. Though the way a sentence is meant can be expressed by an expansion that becomes part of it. As a smile may wide-open a door. Holding the tools in my mouth I struggle uphill, my body so perfectly suspended between my father's push and gravity's pull that no progress is made. As if consciousness had to stay embedded in carbon. Or copy. Between camp and bomb. But if you try to sound feelings with words, the stone drops into reaches beyond fathoms.

I *am* here, she says, I've learned that life consists in fitting my body to the earth's slow rotation. So that the way I lean on the parapet betrays dried blood and invisible burns. My shadow lies in the same direction as all the others, and I can't jump over it. My mother's waves ran high. She rode them down on me as on a valley, hoping to flush out the minerals. But I hid my bones under sentences expanding like the flesh in my years.

Language, he says, spells those who love it, sliding sidelong from word to whole cloth. The way fingers extend the body into adventure, print, lakes, and Dead-man's-hand. Wherever the pen pushes, in the teeth of fear and malediction, even to your signature absorbing you into sign. A discomfort with the feel of home before it grows into inflamed tissue and real illness. With symptoms of grammar, punctuation, subtraction of soul. And only death to get you out.

We must decipher our lives, he says, forward and backward, down through cracks in the crystal to excrement, entrails, formation of cells. And up. The way the lark at the end of night trills vertically out of the grass—and even that I know too vaguely, so many blades and barely sharper for the passing of blindness—up into anemic heights, the stand-still of time. Could we call this God? or meaning?

The suck of symbol, rather, she quotes. Or an inflection of the voice? Let the song go on. And time. My shadow locks my presence to the ground. It's real enough and outside myself, though regularly consumed at high noon. So maybe I should grant the shoot-out: light may flood me too, completely. But it won't come walking in boots and spurs, or flowing robes, and take my hand or give me the finger with the assurance of a more rational being. And my body slopes toward yours no matter how level the ground.

If we can't call it God, he says, it still perches on the mind, minting strangeness. How could we recognize what we've never seen? A whale in through the window, frame scattered as far as non-standard candles. The sky faints along the giant outline, thar she blows under your skin, tense, a parable right through the body that remains so painfully flesh.

So pleasurably flesh, she says, and dwells among us, flesh offered to flesh, thick as thieves, beginning to see. Even the lark's soar breaks and is content to drop back into yesterday's gravity. Which wins out over dispersion, even doubt, and our thoughts turn dense like matter. The way the sky turns deep honey at noon. The way my sensations seem to belong to a me that has always already sided with the world.

That's why thought, he says, means fear. Sicklied o'er with the pale cast. And the feel of a woman. No boundary or edge. No foothold. Blast outspins gravity, breath to temples, gut to throat, propositions break into gasps. Then marriage. The projectile returns to the point of firing. Shaken, I try to take shelter in ratios of dots on a screen.

A narrow bed, she says. Easier to internalize combustion under a hood while rain falls in sheets, glazing a red wheelbarrow for the hell of it. I don't bait fabled beasts to rise to the surface of intonation. But I once watched a rooster mate, and he felt hard inside me, a clenched fist, an alien rock inside me, because there was no thinking to dissolve him. So to slide down, so unutterably, so indifferent.

I don't understand, he says, how manifest destiny blows west with the grass, how the word "soul" floats through the language the way pollen pervades tissue. Worry pivots in the gut, a screeching brake, so scant the difference between mistake and mental disturbance. Is language our cockadoodledoo? Is thinking a search for curves? Do I need arrowheads or dreadlocks to reach my rawest thoughts? A keyboard at their edge?

The longer I watched, she says, the more distinctly did I feel the snap of that shot flat inside me. So simple the economy of nature: space appears along with matter. So to slide down and stand there. Such self-gravity. So narrow the gap between mistake and morning sickness.

I sit in my own shadow, she says, the way my mother gave birth to it. In artificial light, blinds drawn against the darkness of power. I think of you as if you were that shadow, a natural enclosure, a world, not a slight, so I can wander through your darkness. Has our contract inverted time, made our universe contract, a cramped bed for two? And when I say your name, do I draw water, a portrait, curtain, bridge, or conclusion?

Place there is none, he quotes. Not even to hang up our archetypes. Let alone Star-Spangled Banners. We go forward and backward, and there is no place. Therefore it is a name for God. My eye, steadfast on traffic lights, abolishes the larger part of the round world. I should look at my feet. Space sweeps through us, a hell of distances bathed in the feeble glow of emptiness. Outward mobility, unimpeded. Suddenly we're nobody home, without any need of inattention, imposture, or talent for deceit.

The wind whips my skin as if it were water, she says. My skin *is* water. For wind read wind, news, sky falling. Is it a mental disturbance or the higher math of love if I hear you talking under my breath and from the torn fragments assume the sun is far away and small, and a look can cause a burn? Superstition, too, is a kind of understanding, and to forgo it may have consequences.

Clusters of possibilities whiz through our head, he says. Electric charges, clogged highway, screeching brakes, a house too full of guests. With grounds for disagreement and miscarriage. The light rushes in dry, screaming. But the opaque parts of the nerve oppose the noise and void the options. Then the project must be prolonged in terms of lack.

■ ■ ■ ■ ■ ■

INTERLUDE

SONG

long
as in hypnosis
not easeful by half
in love

a white jug with flowers
no room
among pictures
from within

look how even of dreams
we try to make sense

MEDITATION ON FACT

"I know" is supposed to express a relation between me and a fact.

old arteries acquainted with

Where fact is taken into consciousness like your body into mine, and I'm all sponge and crevice, floating heat and sold but for the tiny point where I, instead, give birth to myself.

carrying blood
naturally

Or I stumble after, a beginning skater on thin ice. Or a hawk outlined against the sun brims my eye, the speed of steep descent its evidence.

bewitched by

This picture shows how the light falls, bright as advertising, not what stokes it at bottom. A desire comes legs apart, demanding the color red. While the hawk's plummet smears the gap visible, a scar to be deciphered as force of attraction. Or gravity.

even as far as the foot

So my relation to fact lies deep, deep below the roadbed of inquiry, below the sequence of step and foothold, vowel and consonant, diminishing with distance. Drowned under thin ice. The sun far away and small.

SONG

began gold
in the eyes
wind lifting
sheets

whispered
the classic
texts salt
in your mouth

so to slide
and slice breath

Unreachable, she says, left of the left margin. A moment suspended. As if it didn't apply, didn't invite to bite the apple. Garden caught as in amber by an extra gravitational force. A sphere with the beauty of curved surfaces that seem flat and endless. Though it may crack. Sprung reason, hinge or nail.

Even a bold garden, he says, is already wistful. Like the bisons of the cave paintings, the phallic African gods, the frescos found in Pompeii. As if we could step into an image of what we have lost. Tight fit of pine and apple trees in turf studded with a fine fickleness of morning glories. We're not eagles soaring above, leaving every leaf as it is, but at least we don't fear flying with the sparrows. And multitudes of insects. The explicit sun, or maybe inherent wear, occults our act, and we fall back into the old tale.

Time, she says, on all sides. Without shore. We drown if we set foot in, though we're bound to. As incurably as proton and neutron are bound to the dim world of the nucleus. And once we learn to breathe in the crash of water desire rushes in, takes hold of our smallest gesture as of a sail. But at the edge of the picture we fall. And are born. In all directions.

A common nucleus, he says, but different numbers of double binds. The earth soaks up semen without drawing conclusions. A gloved finger says touch and touch me not. But who could live among ornaments wrought by abstinence? Who could be so thorough?

Don't you think it a strange coincidence, he says, that every man whose skull's been opened had a brain? And as late as 1889, Charles Brown-Sequard, a famous French physiologist, at the age of seventy-two, treated himself for waning vigor with extracts from the testicles of dogs.

What a way to bed hope, she says. With a cherished pedigree. What *I* think strange: every photo of the old house shows wide open shutters when I remember breathing gloom, the light a mere trickle from a child's pail. Of course I know which one to inhabit: memory loves hunting in the dark. The added light only exacerbates the vertigo of inner stairwells. I see you still on the first step, plucking the word "now" out of the dark thick with resistance, as if time too had forbidden chambers.

Bursts the skull, he says, the strong force coupling gluons and quarks. Flings you. And you all interval, all excess aspiring to annihilation, slip of wings, a dragonfly so transparent, so impatient to be kicked out of paradise. But the curve slackens. The crow doesn't fly as the crow flies. And it's no longer unthinkable to put on pants and trace scars on a page.

Do you think there just might be a physiological explanation? she asks. But what happens in the brain if we always relate an object to a certain difficulty? The riddle solved, the dust is supposed to settle. But if the motes keep in motion, the house under water, shadows swimming through like undeveloped photos or the inconsolable dead? A space can have this color even though light ought to be the same to all observers. The frame of memory both distinct and not distinct from looking at photographs in order to remember.

Opens to the touch, he says, you have to feel it, and remains as much a stranger. Fields of sesame split wide. You ride, ribcage abird, toward disappearance, toward a preorganic, duty-free state of body. As if consciousness curved into minerals, and thought, at its peak, were only a shiver.

We are afraid of each other, she says. That's why we find a makeshift mistress, a third to be excluded. Then we think we have cleared the screen, can sit crosslegged inside language and practice passion according to the Russian novel. But something, a thin fear of sundrown, remains between us, measuring the distance as if it were the essence of being close.

Like a color we don't see, but know is contained in the light? he asks. The force that couples or, if weak, revises identity and sex? Measuring distances in the mind refracts emptiness. As if we could touch the infinite when all we do is study our fingerprints on the lens. And the pain, exacerbated toward the red end of the spectrum till we're left to howl on a cosmic scale.

It matters more *how* something touches us, she says, manner more than magnitude. Even your body could bulk foreign into mine. A clinical glitch. Or the light on a clump of cottonwoods might feel like the giddier light over the Moshassuck when you know it flows miles away, or that you could take a walk inside your mind and find me there. The explanations double-lock the strangeness.

We lie in the dunes, she says, drowned between sheets to the wind. Green capped white, the surf's disguise of beginnings, depending on the length of curve observed. If I must have a god I'll take the matter between noun and verb. The nothing that defines, shapes next-to into phrase or cleanliness. Then again, the nothing between the teeth of a comb parts nothing but the nothing between hairs. So maybe I'd rather have an old woman sprawled barefoot through fields and space foam, pushing her breasts at any weed in the world as if the only true way to see were by touch.

An intelligence that comprehends the sperm, he says. Tubes, valves transporting cells toward strange attractors, riot canals through the blood, one-way excess. Once you miss one rung of the ladder you can't stop falling. The hole takes over the argument, pigeons the sky, and the clouds, so calm a moment ago, blush and swim wild with reproduction, albeit asexual.

A space between boundary and blur, she says, a nakedness beyond male and female, edge of the sea. The tongue surrounds the mouth, so that you answer questions I failed to ask or pass sentence that has not been pronounced. The way radiation bathes the entire universe in a feeble glow and thought chases after the receding galaxies at such speed there is no question of a center and the squeeze of gravity becomes mere alibi.

But no ducts to the marrow of the mind, he says, most private part, opaque like a trauma, no fixed address. No field glasses on the firings, the real event, swerve of light. The germ of your thought swimming too deep. Endlessly in ambush, attention dissipates into longing. I listen to my thirst and know incurable's the rule.

■ ■ ■ ■ ■ ■
INTERLUDE

SONG

rush of water
do not mistake
the singular
of my desire

muscle's
memory
and makeshift
mistress

incurable
the rule

MEDITATION ON CERTAINTY

The more a proposition hardens its glassy simplicity tilts all fluids away from the body, all thoughts into sudden white. A paralyzing excess of focus, and you know you'll never marry.

a third
to be excluded

Certainty so cold in the knees the words faint, amputated. The wood dries, the door starts creaking, the darkroom is opened too soon. It is the lowest point gathers. A host on the tip of the tongue equals worse than any pied piper.

here it is always
morning

The house as if you could draw your character from it, incest of immobility and sedentary adventure, breath sealed by sediment of ghosts. So inferred, daylight trickles from a high window the larger the absence of puddles on the floor.

the eye both hungry and
begins to weep

This wider lens restores confusion, fingerprints and weeds. Relations alter. Not just the river, the bed, too, shifts. Your mother takes a lover. Slow oscillation of lips, as between hide and seek, magnetic and field. Speeds red without limit through tree tops, leaves flowing through veins.

fine hard
invisible rain

Hour of glass, pillar of salt. The words come to their senses. It is the lowest point gathers love. Doubt, sometimes called world. It spills your heart.

SONG

we wait for rain
to fall inside
the body
like a presence of gods

so to open
so fire so silk
with fissures between
small words

in a white jug
the stem of a dream

III

ON VARIETIES OF OBLIVION

After bitter resistance the river unravels into the night, he says. Washes our daily fare of war out into a dark so deaf, so almost without dimension there is no word to dive from. Body weight displaced by dreams whose own lack promises lucidity so powerful it could shoot a long take to mindlessness. Fish smell travels the regions of sleep, westward like young men and the dawn. Then I return, too early to bring anything back, unsure of what I want, terrified I'll fail, by a hair, to seize it.

We talk because we can forget, she says. Our bodies open to the dark, and sand runs out. Oblivion takes it all with equal tenderness. As the sea does. As the past. Already it suffuses the present with more inclusive tonalities. Not orchestrating a melodic sequence, but rounding the memory of a rooster on top a hanging silence. Or injured flesh. Impersonal. Only an animal could be so.

An avatar of the holy ghost, he chuckles. Or the angel of the annunciation beating his wings against a door slammed shut. Behind it, love already plays the organ. Without the angel. He is invisible because we have rejected his message.

On the old photos, she says, I see a stranger staking out my skin. As if an apple could fall too far from the tree. Yet I call her "me," "my" years of furtively expanding flesh, with almost-certainty. It's a belief that seems exempt from doubt, as if it were the hinge on which my doubts and questions turn. Still, I may seem the same "I" to you while I've already rolled it through the next door. From left to right.

My separation from the wetlands started even earlier, she says. In my mother's mirror, which staged dialectic on acute unease of body. There are few forest fires in the smoke, or even trains whistling, the station run down. Yet I mourn more friends than waste of trees or bald eagles lost. I carry the mirror in my occipital lobe, but cannot inhabit my womb. The silence between parts. Of speech.

A pebble in an eddy, he says, reveals the course of the current. It's in the flash of dissonance that we know, if not want, each other. A knowledge thick with green sun, parrots, snakes, charmers. Then dissolves in the rush toward the remote. I search for control, but there is only the gap to the horizon, beckoning without event.

Only out of body could we be out of time, she says. Momentarily bracket it maybe, in illness, degrees of withdrawal, flimmer above the lake. But hours reproduce. A lay in time saves the lay of the land and the garbage collects. I can't distinguish gravity from grace or other distortions of space. My now begins six billion years ago, when fish stretched their fins onto dry land, or forty, with breasts and monthly bleeding. Always already darkening, the way a sentence anticipates the period it will stiffen in.

The galaxies avoid collapsing onto each other by virtue of their recessional motion, he says. Father and son walk away from the bed in opposite directions. But sweat clings to our names steamed in the same sleep. If I withdraw to more impermeable regions, the secretions of closeness increase. As if all respiratory passages led to you. As if you were the certainty that a shadow of doubt lengthens. On my lungs.

It would take more than a pebble, she says, to plumb your undertones. Something slips away as you speak, tense with life, a startled beast in the woods. Is it a lizard, snake or bigger game? The brush closes over the trace of flight. A cloven hoof?

Isn't this a case, he says, of deep breathing pulled into spasms of interpretation the way children are pulled into the future by the gravity of their innocence? And with a speed unlimited by the young space. The joints between future and present swell and sweep apart whole galaxies. But even the most intense black still reflects a little light, and history will take care of our rage for explanation.

What if all our thinking, she says, were a search through underbrush and mud. Trying to decipher the forest without artificial light. The rustlings of language give us the illusion of a deep dimension. But our equations don't net the unknown quantity. We're only as good as our words.

Do you mean, he asks, that it's futile to ignore the bright emptiness of symbols and plunge to mine the deep? Illusory or not? The deep of focus? forest? world? the body? Where it is too dark for language to throw its shadow? Where it is not enough to know good and evil, but we must act on it, though it's beyond our strength and will destroy us?

Champollion fainted, she says, once he had wrested their secret from the hieroglyphs and saw them turn transparent. The serpent no longer with power to strike, but biting its tail. I smell my salts, my packets of words, panicked. I'm no longer sure whether they shape my reality or have too little mass to interact with naked matter. Then they would pass right through the earth as I will in death.

The lightest particles gather the energy, he says, and given their density, outweigh stars. Thought follows thought, the interval calibrated on the space between your legs. Your yes fire, your no the crack of a whip. Well, more a filament breaking in a lightbulb. Eating from the Tree of Knowledge can't be undone. Only muddied, as by motivation. And the way you thrust out your belly as you walk, with almost shameless indifference, makes a void in the air, but no case for cosmic deceleration.

So even if I despair of plane surfaces, she says, writing, even talking, becomes an act of faith that my bondage to grammar and lexicon is not in vain. That these symbols in their beautiful and hallucinatory nudity blind me only to make me see. There is fire under the smoke. The sun also rises and falls.

We still read at risk, he says, but we don't need to lard the crocodile with arrows. The picture won't devour us. It is swallowed in the fluid agreements between gonads and frontal lobe at a rate relative to the dark closing in. Yet two speeds in paroxysm need not mesh. A burning heart, failing to strike while hot, may not save the burning feet.

■ ■ ■ ■ ■ ■

INTERLUDE

SONG

fire tied
under your breast
all angles an apple
could fall

distances traveled
a fish to the West
the leaves blue
as the sun

it is your turn
to think

MEDITATION ON UNDERSTANDING

Even if you were to express everything that is "within you," if the flesh opened.

rain curtains
the eye

Or if it could talk, the bold insect on the page I'm reading, a moving violation pushing its smallness to the brink as exemplary economy. Pulled, as if it were one of the letters, into vain sequence by my eyes.

the surface of
a lake

Is it that I can't foresee the way your thought grows into anger? a body? How nudity is yet another garment? Blurred invasion. Can't stand in your shoes, under your wear, over your soul. Thirsty on awakening. Beside the point. The lake overflows without bringing childhood memories up into the light.

ricochets

The rings on the surface announce events already dissolving, the pebble's fluid migrations among contingent waves.

like
lovers

No deep image. A fault line through the lake. I've never dreamed of hunting though I sleep in a cave. The rain goes on falling. Rust in the bones. The riddle need not have a solution, need not be a riddle. Anyone can dream.

SONG

the king with
all his medals
rides horseback toward
the Sacred

Heart adrift
on the same wall
this is
his real life

meaning can take
but two dimensions

IV

ON WAYS OF THE BODY

In important ways, he says, the ways of the body, speaking in one's imagination cannot be compared to crying out loud, or only like tennis with a ball and tennis without one. Yet the games are similar. This is why the idea of another world can still net a sunlit slope when the valley is already dark and we should reach for a glass of wine. Grist of images. But ordinarily I don't think of "inner events" shadowing my speech. Just as I don't worry if my sperm have long or short tails.

And what can writing not be compared to? she asks. Having a ball? A child growing from your long-tailed sperm? A boatload of foreigners climbing the Statue of Liberty, waving flags? The price of deciphering seems to be transparency. Also called fainting. The wings of the dragon-fly are beautiful, but the body is not itself. I want the missing meat, bone, metabolism and ratios of heat and hunger. At the price of windows muddied with fingerprints.

Thinking runs between speech and above pigeonholes, he says, but our one sky falls on the street, leaving puddles. I worry beads between my fingers and how to revive dead letters. Or does a flower out of rubble say less for life than how meager our claims? The image is consumed in the missing detail, the gap of promise. But suddenly a word gets down on all fours and sniffs at your crotch. Or a memory screams on your cheeks while you try to hold on to the edgy afternoon.

The dog, she says. There is always a dog. But this warm flick of a tongue. Grass softer than sleep, and the dog standing over me, panting, penis flaming red from under his yellow coat and crooked as though in pain. Warm flick of tongue on my face. Wet shock. Worried boundary or bone.

Was I frightened by what I saw, she asks, or by my own eyes? Red, crooked penis. Did my hand follow its logic into blindman's buff? Did I learn to read in order to purge incomprehensible desires? A prisoner of memory regenerating in the marrow, the red power of a dog, or the stranger need of language? Missing transport by muscle or metaphor. So that I bite my lip and see beside the point.

Are you saying that greater density attracts more matter? he asks. Of fact? That abstract means distance? That our parents' act has exploded the present indicative? Nothing has ever been deciphered but turned out beasts coupling. Even books spot with secret menstrual blood and propagate their species. My hand forms letters of unambiguous design. Or are you preparing me for new ways of behavior?

Old ways, she says. Though sometimes I feel you less as an animal than huge rampant vegetation taking root inside me, covering my whole world, from top to there's no bottom, with sheer presence. And me almost bursting out of my skin, a drop of water, all surface tension. Now I spread more like a puddle, my body relaxing away from me, no matter how firmly I decline its offers of expansion.

Does it even make sense to say "then" and "now," he asks, when our world expands in every direction away from itself and the speed of light is measured to be the same regardless of how we are moving? Maybe it's the frame that strikes resemblance until the fullness of time allows all forms to dissolve? I know, aging is not an article of a woman's religion. Every night, we cover our nakedness to dry the ink. Every morning the page is as empty as the scene of a crime.

Why is it, she asks, that we cannot share experience, not even under the same sheet? Rain falling or not. That my pleasure in your pleasure is unsteady like decaying atoms or continents mapped on a dream? The light of difference sharper than the warmth of next to or the same wild cucumber vine. We expected pursuit to close on happiness. But it remains pursuit, the happiness intermittent, a meteorite igniting as it passes through our air.

Any text crumbles, he says, even if we approach the tree before the leaves are falling. And the gaps don't let the light show through, let alone the color of quarks. The photographer says smile as if an unease with family likeness could be refocused as identity. In spite of superhuman efforts to keep my dead father's body from encroaching on mine, I am caught, moon in eclipse, an eager atom weighing toward form out of sheer need for anxiety.

Intermittent, she says, as if a space of time, too, could not be occupied by two bodies. Even bodies of experience and memory. As if we had no history, only a past purloined by nothing to show for it. The way I feel robbed in the morning, dreams bleached by the rush of too bright light. A film gone white, with only stray bits of raw dark. The body inhabits those as consciousness inhabits forgetting. And the gap between pain and knowing recloses the way matter comes to in the light.

Our love moved with the slowness of an object, he says. Blueshifted as sitting for a portrait where you can't grudge time. It awakened fingers at the tip of our words, chambers in the heart. Then suddenly everything too close, a splinter under the skin. The model has gotten a cramp, the cat eaten her young. Vertigo of reflections, the smooth surface lost in eddies and currents.

A splinter lodged in the brain, he says, this effort to trap fluctuations in wavelength or feeling. To see not only both duck and rabbit in the puzzle, but to freeze the moment of flip. Or a moment of aging. Is it too subtle, like grass growing, like the size of a proton? Or is our inability more categorical, the way a shadow cannot catch the light, or the eye see its blind spot? Do I love your face because it is yours or because of the way it differs from circle, parabola, ellipse?

Perhaps we need change to see what's there, she says. And ambiguity, to be aware of seeing. Seven types of apples. But focus on the curvature of the lens, and night gains all color, torpor all deeds, even their reflections in the river. Pores stop their doors. The grass is blunt with mass, the sky not infinite, just soot.

So we should not watch each single breath, he asks, but simply take in the world and hold it in our body? With the roots laboring in the ground? with poplars standing straight and stiff in the acid rain? And breath by breath set it down again and not worry how *is* connects with *the case*? Like an acrobat? An acrobat.

There are things, she says, we cannot say. But to keep them down in the body doesn't save us. Even if use equals meaning, nakedness may not rise to the occasion of high noon. Legend says time began when an eagle pierced the sun and was consumed in fire. Moment of transfiguration, sublime and pitiful. The mind suffering sunstroke, overcome by its own light just when it thinks it is defeating the darkness.

SONG

we practice
the body
with moldy bread
with holes in the cheese

so to decipher
or feel
the thinning
under the skin

is there still time to act
on impulse

MEDITATION ON THE INDEFINITE

If a pattern of life is the ground for using a word the way tree bark beds columns of ink, then the word must contain some penumbra, some pulp, some that is never born.

the shape of smoke

Life is, after all, collusion of thick and fast, spacetime foam and Berenice's hair, curving suddens, sand, surds, masses of matter. Nonplussed. No exact exchange. Swords.

muscles endeavor
to shorten

Sharper concepts would not pack lunch. Sharper eyes not see farther than irregularities of wave and too wet. Not their own blind spots. Born as an afterthought I doubt propositions without body heat or shadow.

vague terms

We can predict high-pitched storms, but not the wind's local practice. Opposing thumb and upright imposture. What people will and. Distress blowing cold, inches of slow disguise.

replaced by waves

Polymorph appearances and singular gods. Five is a hand, ten a whole perversion. Pretending to recognize the relatives as if to make amends. For refusing progeny. If our universe.

sets us
guessing a proper
game

SONG

in this country
the orphans
are tall
and pollen is carried by wind

if a girl stands
a baby
hooked to her hip
what takes the place of

little enough
counts the change

v

I used to think, if I were light enough my conjectures would take wing, he says. But it's for the birds, the emptiness in the bone, the compulsion to keep moving: air affords no perch, gravity not neutralized by neighboring particles. And the light stays just beyond the upper left corner, not weighed down into substance by a lead pencil or the ridiculous mouse I expect to give birth to mountains.

"The act of writing weakens the eyes, bends the back, breaks the ribs, cramps the belly. It's a pox on the whole body," said a cranky copyist in the eleventh century, she says. We already carry too much equipment on our back to carry a tune up the mountain, what with thin air. And the weight makes us sluggish to move, even to open our shutters. So there are many things we do not see. And what if we saw the enormous woman collapsed on the sidewalk? We can't leave her lying there. But she is much too heavy to lift.

Odd, he says, how the road to our neighbor tends to run parallel, past her, out into emptiness. I'd like a space where we would *have* to intersect. Or else be hyperbolically myself, alone and too tall. As a book may be a book only if, once the voice has abandoned it along with daylight, it is still worth its candle. I lost my father by following him at a mathematically precise interval. Given how young the universe, you could deliver a child and never recover it.

From birth, she says, we breathe against the mark. Half the girls want to be boys; half the boys, birds. Bright tail feathers over soft lift of flesh. An extra ledge for song, a soar of pleasure to invent the world. Fewer sing every spring. Meanwhile my body expands horizontally, stretching the distance between my breasts to incomprehension.

What if sense disintegrates even though you're stroking my breasts? she asks. If I can't put my arms around you, the gesture hollow like a bad actor's? If words abandon me? If I find emptiness where you find yourself, and it's neither sheltering nor sky? If my eye no longer holds things in the way of a lover, flesh offered to flesh, or even a task? If it shirks and shrinks back into its orb of blind bone, opens and closes only to let empty light travel through?

The steady breeze levels the ridges in the sand, he says. Though it leaves specks of mica. Instead of a handful of world we find too many material structures, even if biodegradable, with flavors strange and charmed. Quarks and leptons proliferate, clouds of gas, polluted light, and dogs fight over the shadow of a bone. Not to mention trademarks and other corporate black magic. Yet the eye's not a black hole, no matter what its color. Uncluttered by things, it sees inward, into the heart. Which of course may also be empty.

Are you telling me there's no hope? she asks, that I'm dark matter that doesn't emit or reflect radiation? Or to clear out the gossip of perception, so even minimal attention can span a paradigm? The way a change of light, or love, can reveal a face? Or erase it? The way the leaden stupor of extreme fatigue can sometimes weigh toward a lucidity so keen it cuts?

Shrinking cores and exploding peripheries, he says. Supernovae, new Crab Nebulae. A stricken star, but, ah, a lovely light, rose window, chandelier. Perhaps light is only the consciousness of the dark? Like the quick, brilliant flash when the sleep cable snaps and leaves us bereft, stripped of we don't even know what, when we would at least hold the promised hand.

I've had no childhood, he says. Small body, yes, small arms, small mouth, small eyes. Small noise of stomach, lips. Small talk. But how greedily my mother loved more iridescent feathers. Tossed into thin air I madly flapped my shimmering identities to nerve fear into buoyancy. But my flutter did not sustain flight. Her rocking did. An interruption, and I fell.

No flight simulation in my childhood, she says. A muted, almost prenatal state with folded membranes, webbed in waiting. A fierce desire, though, to scale the mountains, bald as they were, the craggy blocks of shale and slate, harsh, brittle, all downward pull, crumbling the time I was blind to. They held up a deep space of promise that widened the eye toward horizons of a different color, toward a crucial indifference out of all bounds.

In the first grade I wore a black apron, he says, on which my chalky fingers left their alphabet, so many hieroglyphs that would not be deciphered. It seemed to pull me toward being a girl. When I lifted it over my head, between me and the sun, I became an apprentice blackboard, a smooth slate on which words and things played their shell game.

A girl's space, she says, and I might add, a scientist's, would be more like foam, or sponge, a structure of wormholes and maybe bridges. Not this excess of black and white, of words in profile, with birds' heads pointing the direction to read them. Toward the death of a childhood you remember but can no longer decipher. Only a written language can die, all others disappear without a trace.

ON PATTERN

I wouldn't want to accuse you of imperfection, she says. Your way of looking at things seems to dress patterns, master ceremonies. You walk as through a formal garden, an inner music cadencing your steps, and all paths intersect. Whereas I shlepp on swollen feet, arms scratched by perhaps imagined brambles, through a wilderness where roads disappear, where even riverbeds wander. And the point vanishes.

The point of music is constant vanishing, he says, and don't mistake pattern for paradise. My world seems a random scatter of snapshots pretending innocence rather than an epiphany of face. We want to believe a focus on light clarifies, if at the price of harshness. But a century of looking through the ultimate keyhole has leached the revelation from under covers and drawn blinds. Now all we've got is a bald mountain.

Or, she says, standing here at the foot of the stairs as if they were an exit, maybe *I'm* what's vanishing, to the point of a figment in someone else's story, feverish. Then my arrogant first person singular would limp in a dichotomy of virtual and existence. All I think, so many commas and periods, dry air, an Arabia Deserta of the mind. With a whiff of smoke reserved for the gods. A pain so flawless you stop breathing. Tacit turns, not on the scale of the voice.

When you speak of pain, he says, it remains hidden under the rush of phonemes, less singular than their sequence and seal. But at least the words, showy as flowers flaunting their sexual parts, save us from the eye's illusion of immediate knowledge where, once the lesions examined, the window is undressed and nobody home. In the aftermath, I cannot enter. I carry photos of my absent loves but don't set a place for them at the table.

■ ■ ■ ■ ■ ■

INTERLUDE

SONG

small body small
talk
so adult
a sadness

the song of less birds
maps the land
a ghost of surface
resting on oil rigs

sleep is a stranger's glove
and the cold comes through

MEDITATION ON AWAKENING

The air vibrates with occult alphabets and the sun's rays bend over a book, but the world is dark. Then one day I open my seeing eye, and there is a dog.

morning admits
no impediment

I'm not sure what's to be done with this picture. Or the dog.

a mirror
complicates

Clearly, we must explore. How the eye blinks a ladder out of oblivion and a step beyond, to see the imaginary depth of the mirror invade the body. Where it folds into letter size.

no soft to the touch
without detour

Exquisitely specific antibodies sidetracked by desire. The light turns to matter, the metaphor gray. The body, jubilant to meet its double, bites into the apple.

upper limit speed

The Book open in the middle of the kitchen will protect the house from lightning. The dog will burn.

though to consciousness
nothing
can happen

The pictures seem to save us work, check the sentence through to the period. But will it wait into the small hours? For words to fall into my mouth, fresh snow on snow already fallen?

SONG

What is the
key of loss?
A face
erased?

absence
so porous
only a woman
can inhabit

sun far away and small
the water in the jug evaporated

VI

Even if our life seems scattered, a text always going astray, it builds on constants, she says. Like a piece of music. The mind should be able to embrace it in its full extravagance and touch the architecture of cause even as it forms. More so with the years, with resources of slowness. You must sit in a blue shift to sort seed from going to.

Not sit, he says. Arrows toward new setting out even as the day sets. It's in walking, albeit more slowly, that I find where I need to go, just as following the seduction of one basic rule can unknot the dimensions of a whole system. When I try to pace my breath's hovering potential with the wind, particles form into perspective and ride out into the large. I charter a ship, then try to understand what I had in mind.

You launch exotic birds, she says, and some adapt to the Rhode Island winter. I stick with domestic varieties, crows in my face, a rooster on the brain, maybe a Rhode Island Red. Such simple desire blasting the bones electric, so matter of fact, to perch on crags and cliffs. But highs are only one element of the climate. The shadow of a cloud, and my breasts droop, faintly mournful. The sun drops. The surface of the leaves turns blue.

Cells rust, he says, not hunger. It seems yesterday that, gasping with shock, I plunged into the January river for the unreachable that is promised—though only as long as we have no history. Now the train's speed is hostage to the next station, becalmed legs and thinning hair. Could it be that loss completes possession? Becomes, like the "with" in "without," a second acquisition, deeper, wholly internal, more intense for its pain?

Take the hordes of children, she says. So to take off on the crest of light, so to dash toward the horizon through bushes and knee-high grass, undeterred by stop signs, fences or decapitated statues. As if waking were as liquid and hospitable as sleep. As if games didn't close into fist-fights. As if innocence were forever, though time might age, and whole seasons forget to be born.

Even children, he says, toss their pebbles across the river to throw off some undefined unease that weighs on them. As does the indifference the stones drop into. But for a moment their call and echo from bank to bank barely touch the water, skip as on light, as into regions of enhanced density, ever increasing in power.

So was it war or games or clockwork that sped our growing up? she asks. Or simply the way particles behave in a field of force? One day the girl disappears into a different point of reality, a woman with sagging breasts. And still my sense of self remains woolly as in sleep, as if the years had only heaped on more blankets. I always want to hear the sirens, albeit tied to the mast, but I fear becoming the sailor with ears plugged, just plugging away at the oar.

Penelope isn't part of your scenario? he asks. No needlework to undo the fire feeding on our cells? Your woolly self still makes me get under the blankets. But I too want to get down, through the roar and twang, to the deep horizon note I know is there though I can't hear it: my own frequency, my way of being in the world. Is this another image that holds me captive? So deep in the grain I have no way to reach it? And if I could? I once saw a dog stray into the subway and hit the live rail.

I step into my mother's room, she says, and though a woman's body is a calendar of births and injunctions to death, time disappears. Only dead enough to bury could prove sound to silence or the anxiety I know by heart and lung. In my mother's room. The tie between us anticipates any move to sever it. Terror and lack of perspective. The river runs clear without imparting its clarity, whether we step into it or not.

Deep in the bones, he says. If a butterfly fluttering its wings in China can cause a storm in Rhode Island, how much more the residues of radiation, family resemblance and past rituals. The stove glows red. Thin apple trees line the road. You think you are taking a clean sheet of paper, and it's already covered with signs, illegible, as by a child's hand.

The heart has its rhythm of exchange, she says, without surplus or deficit. Mine murmurs your name while conjugating precise explosions with valves onto the infinite. I take it down with me, in the body, to develop in a darkroom of my own. The way the current elongates our reflection in the river and seems to carry it off.

A death without corruption is the promise of photography, he says. Focus and light meter translating a cut of flesh into a tense past laughing its red off. But the film's too clear. Even if smudged with fingerprints. Even if the light falls into the arms of love.

There are many invisible borders, she says. Some erect and inexorable like death or when a lover recedes into friend. But how we fuss as we approach the millennium, after having dozed in its secular sense so long. As if civilization were drawing its lazy length up into a moment of moments, where Human-Nature-Can/Cannot-Be-Changed would slide down opposite slopes of time. The horizon is a function of eye-level. Are we not nose to the ground, overestimating things Christian?

A frame supports what would, on its own, collapse, he says. When I say "book" you don't think clay tablets, silk scrolls, or palm leaves strung together. And deep focus can make the ground turn figure the way light is the coming-to of the dark. In retrospect. Like a German sentence that comes clear only once you reach the verb at its end. By a strong effort of will. Time divides us into dust, but also binds our bodies forward. Though the exhaustion will not be squared.

The moon is constant, she says, my bleeding, a calendar. The instant we apprehend an end we desperately predict new wagon trains to head West, as if adding zeros could create bluer skies and more self-evident truths. As if the universe could big-bang again. And again. When even the most moderate increase in gravity would, instead, make it disappear. Too many dots per inch. Machinery whirring while the credit's gone.

Writing pulls East, he says, like the ground under our feet. For all our love of speed we cling to the slower proofs measured in mutations, milky ways, and ever the wind blows. Poof. The spectacle inside the eye projects its large rhythm onto a trust in daybreak. Which we make ours. Because as long as we follow we lag behind, and the centuries pass intestate.

■ ■ ■ ■ ■ ■

ACKNOWLEDGMENTS

Grateful acknowledgment is made to the editors and publishers of magazines and journals in which sections of these books first appeared:

THE REPRODUCTION OF PROFILES: *Acts, Brooklyn Review, Central Park, Cold Water Business, Conjunctions, Constant Red/Mingled Damask, Feminist Studies, Gallery Works, Grosseteste Review, HOW(ever), In Folio, New American Writing, Ninth Decade, O·blēk, Oovrah, Open Places, Reality Studios, Sink, Southpaw, Temblor,* and *Tyuonyi.*

LAWN OF EXCLUDED MIDDLE: *Big Alice, Blue Mesa, Chelsea, Conjunctions, Epoch, fragmente, furnitures, Hambone, New American Writing, Notus, O·blēk, Raddle Moon, Sojourner, Temblor,* and the *UCSD Archive Newsletter.*

The author would like to thank the Fund for Poetry for a grant.

RELUCTANT GRAVITIES: *Bathos Journal, Black Bread, Boxkite, Conjunctions, Colorado Review, Diacritics, Denver Quarterly, Five Finger Review, Inscape, New American Writing, Ohio Review, Rhizome,* and *Sulfur.*